Diane Z. Hawksford is the owner and developer of The Diagnostic Center of Learning Patterns, Inc. As an R.N., with a Bachelor of Science in Health Arts and a M.A. in Gifted Education Curriculum, she has long been interested in the research aspect of neurological conditions. Diane chose this book as the second to be published from her resource center as it relates to her most favorite role in her own life; that of being a mother to her three children, and grandmother to their children, but especially in the context of counting one's blessing for a healthy child. Hopefully the story of Beverly Gelhaye's loving tenacity and devotion to her handicapped daughter will be an inspiration to all mothers everywhere.

By the same author and also published by the Diagnostic Center of Learning Patterns, Inc.

Polio: A Special Ride
Audio Book: *Diane's Point of View*
                A 90 minute treatise poem about identity.
CD: Memories: Compositions of Love by Diane Z.
CD: Holiday Wishes by Diane Z. and Ron Z.
Tape: Puppet on a String by Ron Zemke

Upcoming Books:
Alzheimer's: Lost in Another World Forever
Diane's Point of View: 90 minute identity poem in book format.

Upcoming Poems:
A Tired Old Mom
A Tired Old Dad

Special Note from the Publisher

This book is intended as a personal story of real life experiences as Beverly Gelhaye remembered. The research is based on the bibliography as listed. This was written for and is intended for cerebral palsy victims, their families, and caregivers everywhere.

The research references were taken from a variety of professional opinions, but this book is not intended to replace professional advice that any individual would have at their disposal from their own experienced practitioner.

A proper personal assessment and diagnosis from one's own experienced practitioner is always recommended before trying any of the treatments outlined in this book.

Cerebral Palsy

She Didn't Cry

A nurse's real life story of one mother's real life experience with cerebral palsy and its life-long ramifications in and through her daughter.

Diane Z. Hawksford, R.N.,
B.S.H.A., M.A. Gifted Education
Curriculum

The Diagnostic Center of Learning Patterns,
Inc., DCLP
Minnetonka, Minnesota

First Published in the USA in 1997 by The Diagnostic Center of Learning Patterns, Inc. Minnetonka, Minnesota 55305

Cover design by The Diagnostic Center of Learning Patterns, Inc.

Final Editing by Pam Hutton, B.A., English, with assistance by Laura Skoglund, R.N. and Ron Zemke, brother, writer and composer.

Printed and bound in the USA by Geehan Graphics

Library of Congress cataloging in publication data available.

ISBN 1-891421-03-4

ACKNOWLEDGMENTS

This story is a true love story, in my view, as only a mother's love has carried me through all these years. I wish to thank first of all Diane Hawksford for being my avenue of expression. Our work together has broadened my knowledge, opened my mind, and allowed me to change in ways I never dreamed possible. I even managed to impress my father!

In looking back over these twenty five years I must acknowledge Fraser School once again for taking Melissa into their school at such a young age and developing her strengths. I wish to also acknowledge Mary Lou Smith, a wonderful teacher at Michael Dowling School, Eloise Friend with the Alumni Girl Scouts of Richfield, Minnesota, Faith and Light of Richfield, Minnesota, Opportunity Partners where Missy works, and for my Missy, her dear friend Cheryl Kock who passed away three years ago and left such a void in Missy's heart.

I also wish to thank all our friends and family who have listened to me all these years, and the patient and loving people up at Webb Lake who have made Missy feel as special to them as she is to us.

Beverly Gelhaye

7

THE BIRTH OF A HANDICAP
MENTAL RETARDATION
CEREBRAL PALSY

She didn't cry!!! My longed for baby girl was born, and she didn't cry. Instead of happy voices and exclamations of joy there was silence in the delivery room. I can remember vividly wondering why she didn't cry. Wondering why everyone was so silent. Wondering why I felt so cold and alone. As if it were a premonition of cold and lonely days to come, I lay there wondering why they didn't bring my baby girl to me so I wouldn't feel so cold and alone. My Melissa Marie. The girl I had waited for so long. Why couldn't I hold her? See her?

The separation was exacerbated by the way the medical personnel in the delivery room surrounded her, while I lay at a distance, unable even to see her. I've often wondered if the coldness I felt at that time was from a physical basis or an emotional one of separation. An inkling, a feeling, everything was not right with my baby. Yet I could not find the words or the energy to ask if my baby was okay. I didn't ask, and no-one offered a word of comfort, encouragement, or congratulations to me.

With my prior two deliveries being a long ten and twelve years before, I began to wonder if I had forgotten so much or if things had changed so much? Maybe babies didn't cry so lustily at birth now with new techniques in delivery as I remembered my sons doing? Hopefully there was some simple explanation why Melissa Marie wasn't crying, and why I was experiencing feelings of fear that I had not felt before? Maybe when I got warm I would realize this was all a silly notion. I was so cold!!!

Time was standing still. Everything was happening in slow motion. It was as if I was watching a production, rather than being a part of a production. The next thing I remember was being wheeled down the hallway to my room in silence. Even my husband's face seemed

8

obscured from my view, making my feelings of separation and aloneness even more pronounced.

Finally, after what seemed an eternity, they brought Melissa Marie to me. I was so happy to see her beautiful face that I never looked any further to see if she was okay. I never checked to see if all her fingers and toes were there. What could possibly be missing when she had such a beautiful face? What could be wrong with this bundle of joy that looked every bit the normal healthy baby? I pushed my suspicions aside and simply allowed myself to concentrate on bonding with this beautiful girl of mine. Wasn't bonding between mother and child the most important emotion to begin feeling at this time? In retrospect, this lack of defining the idea of a truth in my mind, made acceptance of the difficult truth I had to accept, years later, even harder to define. Now I can see that, but I doubt anyone could have convinced me of that at the time.

Melissa Marie was diagnosed with mild cerebral palsy by a neurologist when she was thirty months of age. She is now twenty five years old, and because I have lived with cerebral palsy for so many years, I want to share with you what I have learned. I learned over the years that medical experts are unable to agree about what causes cerebral palsy in children who have congenital CP, but they do know that the child who is at highest risk for developing cerebral palsy is the premature baby who does not cry in the first five minutes after delivery, or needs to be on a ventilator for over four weeks, or has bleeding in the brain. Melissa Marie was not premature, but she did not cry. I was correct in wondering why. The diagnosis of cerebral palsy was attained actually, in the end, through the assistance of a physical therapist who questioned Melissa's pervasive muscle rigidity.

Muscle rigidity, which we learned over the years can be manifested in a variety of ways in each specific cerebral palsy case, should have been the first clue to someone, I

9

think, that something was amiss. If anyone suspected anything, they certainly didn't speak up. Perhaps that all-pervading silence that surrounded Melissa Marie's birth remained at work for a long time. No one really wants to be the bearer of bad news, I suppose. Does it harken back to the days when the messenger was shot if someone was distressed by bad news?

To my mind today, the rigidity manifested itself so clearly in the way she laid on her back, arching herself as if trying to find a more relaxed position, or one of comfort and relief. I remember thinking she was stretching her little body, when in reality she was posturing in an abnormal way. I caught myself more than once staring at her as if in a dream trying to remember if I had ever seen my other two babies move in that manner. She would twirl her tiny hands around in a circular motion in the oddest manner, and that - I was sure - was different, but still neither I, nor anyone close to me, including the professionals, said a word. Of course, I did not ask either and I have learned the hard way that if you do not ask the right question you do not get the right answer. Why didn't I ask? Who wants to be the first to put forth the idea that there is something wrong, perhaps very wrong, with a baby? That premonition I felt in the delivery room was perhaps pushed out of my mind but hung very heavily still in my heart. How could I verbalize the pain that would accompany the full knowledge of a diagnosis that would signify the loss of a dream? The loss of a healthy baby, the reality of a handicapped adult for life.

DENIAL: A WONDERFUL SHOCK BREAKER

Denial is a wonderful shock breaker. It surrounds you like a pillow, causing you to want to sink further and deeper into it until you almost fall asleep in the warmth of your self-imposed trance. Who would want to wake up and be faced with the reality of a child who will remain a child, dependent upon you forever? So let me sleep with my coveted pillow until I'm ready and willing to give it up, Dear World. Give me that, will you please?

The problem with denial in cerebral palsy is that tomorrow comes immediately and daily. It seemed like every day of her young life Melissa was faced with a new struggle for her and our whole family. As I watched my new daughter, my respect and love for her grew by leaps and bounds, seeing her meet the challenges of her life so valiantly. Even as a baby she would smile and laugh so easily. A bundle of joy that transcended the dark cloud that hung ever so ominously near by, always threatening to rain on her parade. We all clung to our umbrella, that was conveniently turned upside down, so as to hold the negative vibes of cerebral palsy at arms length as long as possible. Finally when you can't deny the truth any longer you have to take off your rose colored glasses and see things more clearly.

Melissa Marie's decreased muscle tone was causing her trouble in sitting, she was unable to keep her trunk stable enough so that she could use her arms and legs. In other words, Melissa Marie could not support positions on her own without help. Finally our umbrella of denial overflowed, and we had to start absorbing the full implication of what a diagnosis of cerebral palsy means to everyone involved....

In the United States today, more people have cerebral palsy than any other developmental disability, including Down's syndrome, epilepsy, and autism. About two children out of every thousand born in this country have

11

some type of cerebral palsy. These problems include mental retardation, seizures, language disorders, learning disabilities, vision and hearing problems.

In Melissa's chain of continually surfacing movement problems, was this ever present, all-pervasive lack of fluid body movement. Even as a new baby, she could not suck on the nipple of her bottle in an even motion. Her rigid clamping down sucking motion would cause her to consume more than she could swallow and would cause her to choke very easily. This scared my poor husband more than anything else at that time. Her extremely deep palate still causes her difficulty at times when she is eating, and she is twenty five years old, but as a baby the rigidity of her movements seemed to cause her the greatest difficulty.

Cerebral palsy is actually the term used for a variety of disorders that affect a child's ability to move and maintain posture and balance. To complete a movement smoothly, the tone in all muscle groups involved must be balanced. The brain is responsible for sending messages to each muscle group to actively change its resistance, and in cerebral palsy these messages simply do not achieve that smooth balance that most of us take so much for granted.

THE MAGIC OF MUSCLE TONE IS THE BRAIN

Pediatricians, neurologists, and therapists working with the sufferers of cerebral palsy as a disorder of movement and posture, classify the specific cases according to their "muscle tone differentiation." Muscle tone is what enables us to sit with our backs straight and our heads up. Muscle tone allows us to bend our arms in order to bring our hands up to our face. In short, muscle tone is the miracle of movement that is a body moving in a fluid, smooth, balanced way. Like the figure skater that can fly through the air as if moved by some magical force, muscle tone allows completion of all movements however simple, by its magic of balanced tone in all the muscle groups involved simultaneously. The magic of muscle tone is the brain. The brain is responsible for sending the messages to each muscle group to attain this balance by actively changing the resistance. To bend your arm to bring your hand up to your face, you must shorten or increase the tone of the biceps muscles on the front of your arm while at the same time lengthening or reducing the tone of the triceps muscles on the back of your arm. All this happens in the "normal" scope of things without a thought, for most people. In cerebral palsy, these movements do not occur in balance, because there are injuries to the brain which interferes with the nervous system working in such harmony.

The wonderful, amazing body can make complicated feats look so easy when everything works in balance, when indeed it is truly a miracle every time we raise a glass to our lips and take a drink. All children with cerebral palsy have damage to the area of the brain that controls muscle tone. As a result, they may have increased muscle tone, reduced muscle tone, or a combination of the two (variable or fluctuating tone). Which parts of their bodies are affected by the abnormal muscle tone depends upon where the brain damage occurs.

13

Medial Sagittal Section of Brain Stem, Cerebrum + Cerebellum

Cerebrum

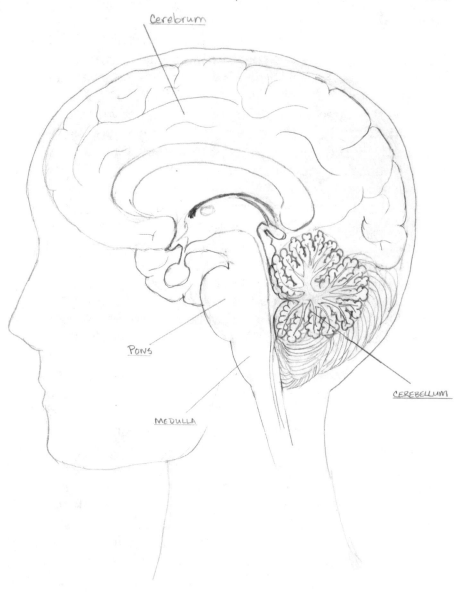

Pons

MEDULLA

CEREBELLUM

CEREBRAL PALSY: A BRAIN PROBLEM

Melissa was well into her teens before I fully realized, or understood the concept that it was her brain's problem and not her legs, back, or arms specifically that were at fault. It was never completely explained to me or my husband where the etiology or cause of cerebral palsy originates in the child. This lack of full understanding of the diagnosis of cerebral palsy leads many an individual involved with the child down the road of misconception, in my estimation. A proper analysis and direction of care, and analysis of treatment towards improvement of the condition, I believe, is tied into this understanding of the condition. In my opinion, the child's chances of recovery, or at least achievement of some measure of their potential and chances for a higher quality of life, is dependent upon this understanding. I am saying, "I wish I would have known then, what I know now."

Regardless of what we knew, or didn't know, the relentless fact of Melissa's diagnosis made itself clear to us, day by day. As Melissa's movement problems became evident in her lack of mobility, ability to explore her environment, and seeming lack of curiosity and motivation to even try to move, we began to seek out further medical advice. Her lack of motivation, as some professionals saw it at first, was turned back to us through such questions as, "Are you handing her things thereby taking away her motivation to get them herself?" Were we at fault because Melissa could not sit or crawl and just wanted to lay there? Amazing, in retrospect, that we even considered the possibility of our guilt, when the natural, normal curiosity of a child spurs them on without any prodding from their parents in most cases. When the brain is involved, someone else's brain, I guess most people look to the reasons for the behavior, or lack of behavior, in the environment first. Brain injury is such a mystery as it manifests itself, that perhaps the answers are so elusive that all possible solutions or reasons must be looked at.

MENTAL RETARDATION: A HARD PILL TO SWALLOW

Finally, when Melissa was 18 months of age we were told she was simply mildly retarded, and we should not expect more of her than would be possible for her to achieve. At most, we were told, she would be capable as an adult of writing a very simple letter in the words of an eight year old. I imagined her writing in the form of Dick and Jane books I had in the first grade as a child. What a bleak outlook!!! We left that medical establishment on a positive note that day only because my husband said, "There is no way they can tell, at 18 months, what a child is capable of by having them stack blocks."………

I read somewhere that, in general, children with mental retardation learn new skills more slowly than other children and find it harder to learn advanced skills such as reading, math, and complex problem solving. Children with mental retardation also may not be as motivated to learn new skills, as are other children. However, this does not mean that children with mental retardation cannot learn. With the above premise in mind, infant stimulation was recommended for Melissa. The purpose of infant stimulation was to stimulate her young brain as much as possible, thereby hoping to increase her intelligence level to the highest potential. We began to seek out a school for her that had a program that could accomplish this for her. This recommendation led us to the Fraser School, and so Melissa was in school at 18 months of age. This was certainly something the two older boys never had the privilege of - school at 18 months.

My little Melissa, in her pink snowsuit, propped between other students in a school vehicle, with eyes as big as saucers looking at me through the window, was off to school. My memory of her that day was like a rebirth of the memory the day she was born. "She didn't cry." I remember thinking what in the world was going to happen next, and why wasn't she crying when I was? Melissa doesn't have the same kind of apprehension that most children would have had because the future is not something she really understands, even now. The future is something of a mystery to all of us, but especially to those who cannot imagine tomorrow and must live in the moment. Even today she will say, "I'm bored now, what do we do next?" In some way it may be a blessing in disguise as the full impact of what they are missing isn't there either, so the pain of knowing what is lost is not ever present with them. She registers pain more through my own eyes than her own, so sometimes I feel I experience the pain for two people.

PRIMARY LABELS VS SECONDARY LABELS

Melissa's primary disability was cerebral palsy, not mental retardation. But mental retardation was the first label placed on my daughter, and the diagnosis of cerebral palsy did not come until almost 12 months later. This confusion in the order of the diagnosis, I believe, had some far reaching effects on everyone subsequently involved in Melissa's plan of care. For myself it seemed like the diagnosis went with the body part involved. Initially when she was just mentally retarded, it was in her brain, and then when she had cerebral palsy, the diagnosis seemed to leave her brain for me and enter her body. Don't ask me why, but suddenly it was those limbs of hers that were totally responsible for not moving properly. Her legs took on a personal character and had a personality all their own. Melissa's legs were just stubborn, I thought. If she could just make those stubborn legs move she would be okay..... Melissa was finally trying to crawl, but do you think those stubborn legs would cooperate? She was actually hopping like a frog instead of crawling, because those legs would not move. Amazing to watch my beautiful little Melissa be so proud of herself because she was moving and crawling the only way she knew how, and I was devastated because she looked like a "frog" - maybe I should say a "tadpole." Even when she would fall flat on her face hopping like a frog, and even breaking a tooth now and then, she was so proud of her movement that you had to admire her courage. So quick to smile, and laugh... Melissa was at least trying to move and that was improvement within the parameters of cerebral palsy.

CEREBRAL PALSY: NOT A PROGRESSIVE DISORDER

One enormous concept that I was never made to understand about cerebral palsy, that I believe is all important, is that it is a static disorder of the brain not a progressive disorder. I believe understanding that concept would have been the most helpful aspect of all to me over the years. Being a static disorder rather than a progressive one, means that the disorder or disease process will not get worse as time goes on. Nor are the motor disorders associated with cerebral palsy temporary, so children with temporary motor problems do not have cerebral palsy and likewise motor problems that get worse over time are not a result of cerebral palsy. Children with cerebral palsy have many other kinds of problems (including medical problems, not all of which are related to brain injury) but most of them are neurological in nature. They do, however, include epilepsy, mental retardation, learning disabilities, and attention deficit hyperactivity disorder. By diagnosing Melissa as mentally retarded prior to diagnosing her with cerebral palsy, somehow the cart got placed ahead of the horse, so to speak, and my constant fear was the progressiveness of her disability. It was my companion constantly. Every day I wondered if she was going to get worse today, or tomorrow, or next week? Could I handle watching her slowly go down hill day by day? Not understanding the non-progressive nature of cerebral palsy added an additional burden to my life that I feel was unnecessary. It eroded my hope, and scattered my view, I believe, of Melissa, and definitely had an effect on her overall level of functioning throughout the years. Many factors; such as the child's attitude toward her disability, the support you provide for your child, and the medical, educational, and therapeutic care the child receives are under the parent's control, and this control can only be recognized if the full concept of the disability is understood by that parental influence.

The Truth Of Cerebral Palsy For Melissa Was In Her Cerebellum

To understand any situation that we are faced with in life, is to come to a full firm mental grasp, a comprehension, so to speak, of the fact or truth of that situation. The full truth of what had gone awry in Melissa's brain was fully diagnosed by an MRI (Magnetic Resonance Imaging) when she was between eleven and twelve years old. Melissa's cerebellum, or little brain as it is sometimes called, had simply never grown. Her little legs were not at fault at all. All the prodding and scolding in the world would not have moved those legs. How I wish I would have understood that sooner. An understanding of the full concept of the inherent problems involved in cerebral palsy over time would have helped me to realize the power I was going to have to maintain, to problem-solve for Melissa all of her life. It is natural that the people who are together the most, and care the most about one another, are going to know what is needed in each other's life, and it would have been helpful to realize that in some cases I knew more than the specialists. This power of understanding would then have allowed me to control what I could control in her life, and let go of what I could not control. Instead I tried for years to hold on to everything so that she wouldn't get worse, and possibly even be cured if I could only find the right answer. I tried everything. I was determined to stop this invisible enemy that had taken over Melissa's body, and our whole lives. The rest of the family was put on hold, so to speak, while the mother and wife in this family was fighting cerebral palsy. I was at war with an invisible enemy in my own home!!!!!!

AT WAR WITH AN INVISIBLE ENEMY:
FIRST WEAPON, CARROT JUICE

One approach I used to fight the enemy was a holistic approach that involved drinking carrot juice. This approach was recommended to me by a friend of our neighbor's who said that carrot juice would work on Melissa's muscles in some mysterious way to relax them. Melissa <u>was</u> to drink carrot juice, so Melissa <u>drank</u> carrot juice until her little hands turned orange. This only took two weeks, but for those two weeks I was at the store every day buying carrots, as it <u>had</u> to be "fresh carrot juice." Had to be natural, and had to be fresh, so I put fresh carrots in a borrowed juicer every day for Melissa to drink. She drank it without a sound. I personally couldn't get a glass down, but maybe that was because I was sick of carrots by the time they were juice. The pulp that came out of the carrots was amazing. I've always thought it was such a waste to just throw the pulp away, but by that time I was sick of both the juice and the pulp. Even Melissa's birthday was celebrated with carrot juice and angel food cake, as she could not spoil the effect of the carrot juice with a "real" cake, and all that "sugar." To this day Melissa will not eat angel food cake, and after a month as the orange color was progressing up her arms, we decided enough was enough...

SECOND WEAPON: VIBRATIONS FROM ENGLAND

Then came information about a man in England who could send vibrations across the ocean, and somehow stimulate Melissa's brain to function more normally. Apparently he had the power to reach Melissa's pineal gland in her brain through these vibrations, with a combination of vitamins and minerals that we were to obtain on this side of the ocean (Texas specifically). However, due to some transportation problems iin the real world, we could never get all of the vitamins and minerals needed, so of course his vibrations could not do the job. We did however send our money off to England for his vibrations (which we could not see or feel) <u>twice</u> before we woke up and "smelled the roses." We had been taken, but a least our daughter hadn't turned another color from this venture.

MELISSA MARIE: A CHILD, NOT A DISABILITY

We, or I should say I, finally tired of looking into a one-way mirror where I only saw myself. I finally began to realize that I was so consumed with Melissa's disorder and my reaction to her handicap, that I was losing all my ability to focus on Melissa herself. I was seeing a disorder, not a child. My husband, I think, knew what was happening all along, but just let me run until I ran out of steam and was ready to focus on the real issue. I couldn't fix it. I couldn't change it. I couldn't run and hide, because Melissa was there. Melissa was everywhere. Her acute sensory system followed me everywhere. Her eyes, which needed correcting at fourteen months, now looked straight at me, and into me. I was an open book to my own child, more than I was to myself. Melissa, to this day, even though she has never been able to communicate verbally in full sentences, through her body language and commanding tone of voice in one word statements, always lets you know what she needs and wants.

EXTRA-SENSORY BEING: OUR MELISSA MARIE

I must say that I now believe in the concept: with a loss there is always a gain. We are so in tune with each other, Melissa and I, that Melissa can almost read my mind, and I most assuredly read hers. It is scary at times. I also realize now that it is the rest of the world that is out of step with the Melissa's of the world, and not vice versa. These children bring a dimension to reality that is impossible to explain to someone who has had no experience with these extra-sensory beings. Experience is the best teacher after all. After twenty five years with my daughter, I now know that experience takes time and a lot of work to acquire, but at that time I was younger and wanted a quick answer, like most young mothers do. Life after all, is life, not a day or a year, but life worked out a day at a time, and when I realized that concept fully I could finally begin to work on a life with Melissa <u>and</u> cerebral palsy. Not a life sentence, but a life filled with learning and loving our special daughter in a special way. I was ready to begin learning about cerebral palsy, and through knowledge turn that one way mirror into a two way mirror. I could begin the process of looking deeper and deeper into that mirror, and see ever more clearly a full illumination of the meaning of cerebral palsy in our child. Seeing and ever following that image of Melissa, the Melissa that was still in her despite the cerebral palsy, would help me to understand the ramifications of the disorder in her, not someone else but our own special little daughter. That real image of Melissa, after all, is the strength of her person, not the weaknesses or handicaps. In other words, I finally began to "accentuate the positive," and "eliminate the negative." Not what she could not do, but what she could do.

NURSE FRIEND'S INFORMATION ON THE EFFECTS OF CEREBRAL PALSY IN THE BODY

How would and how could cerebral palsy possibly affect my child? Cerebral palsy is an affliction with a variety of etiologies or causes. It is somewhat the mysterious enemy I suspected it to be early on, in that the term covers such a variety of developmental neuromotor disorders that the actual site of injury in the brain is often obscured, or at least identified in so few cases that no one wants to go out on a limb and tell you exactly what is wrong or where it is wrong. In that same context no one explains what strengthening processes can be taught in their entirety to the child, as they aren't sure enough of the cause or able to pinpoint the where of the site of injury, and so lose sight of a comprehensive care plan for the cerebral palsy victim. This care plan must cover many years, it seems to me, and must encompass what is known and not known in some logical fashion. Vibrations from across the ocean seemed to make as much sense to my husband and I, at times, as the little bits of fragmented direction we were getting from the professionals. At least, we were sure the vibrations were coming from England, not some unknown planet of **Theory. Einstein's theory of relativity** came to mind at times, as the real full impact of living with cerebral palsy seemed only relative to those "IT" was affecting. "IT" was cerebral palsy, a neuromotor disorder to the professionals, whereas "IT" was Melissa with a neuromotor disorder to us. It was a she, not an it, as she was a very personal entity to us. If we would have allowed "IT" to be otherwise, "IT" would have continued to be the mysterious enemy with no location in Melissa's body. Could it move? Could it leave one part of her body and enter another?

Mysteries always frightened me, and so I began to look and seek out knowledge of what actually happened in Melissa's body? When the MRI confirmed that her cerebellum had not grown, I began to study and ask a nurse friend for information about what the cerebellum is supposed to do in an ordered body. If Melissa had a disorder, then what does order mean in the **idea** of body function? What would a non-developing cerebellum cause over time in her life? Looking at it through Melissa's body, but not taking over her entire being, finally made cerebral palsy real and personal for the first time in years and no longer a mysterious enemy.

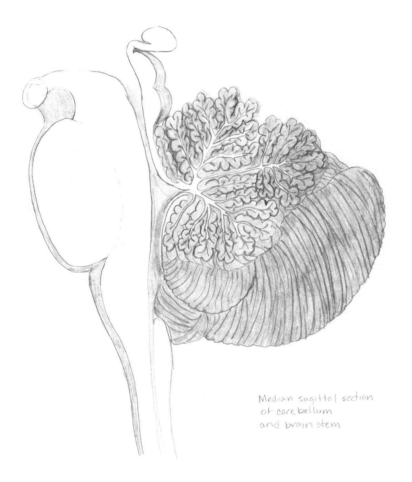

Vestibulocerebellum

Spinocerebellum

Cerebrocerebellum

Median sagittal section
of cerebellum
and brain stem

CEREBELLLUM: THE LITTLE BRAIN

What does the cerebellum do in an ordered nervous system? The cerebellum receives input from many parts of the nervous system, but its output reaches only those parts that are important for the control of movement, both voluntary and involuntary. Functionally the cerebellum can be divided into three zones:

> 1. the **vestibulocerebellum**, which chiefly helps to maintain equilibrium and synchronize head and eye movements,
> 2. the **spinocerebellum**, which orchestrates the muscle activity responsible for limb movements of the kind needed to stuff a coat into an overhead rack,
> 3. and the **cerebrocerebellum**, which plays a role in the planning of movement.

This complex coordination between brain and muscles which is called synchronization, falls largely to the cerebellum, which makes up more that 10% of the brain's weight and contains **nearly half of all its neurons**. The cerebellum receives a wealth of input to perform these tasks. Processing this information automatically and unconsciously, it compares motion instructions from the cerebral cortex with movements in progress, optimizing them as needed. It also appears from research conducted at the University of Minnesota, the activity of the cerebellum is involved somehow in problem solving. "From a study done on seven healthy men who placed their heads in a giant MRI machine," as the article stated, "while doing simple tasks, the flurry of activity in the cerebellum increased." Of course, we're not sure what would have happened with seven females in the MRI machine, but apparently there is some evidence that at least seven men do think with their cerebellum to some extent.

The cerebellum maintains the body's sense of balance by combining information from the inner ear (balance receptors) with sight and position sense. Damage to the cerebellum through trauma or disease creates symptoms involving skeletal muscles. The effects are on the same side of the body as the damaged side of the cerebellum, because of a double crossing of tracts within the cerebellum. There may be then, because of injury, a lack of muscle coordination, called **ataxia** (a=without; taxis=order). Blindfolded people with ataxia cannot touch the tip of their nose with a finger because they **cannot** coordinate movement with their sense of where a body part is located. Another sign of ataxia is a changed speech pattern due to uncoordinated speech muscles. Cerebellar damage may also result in disturbances of gait (staggering or abnormal walking movements such as jumbled movements versus coordinated upward and downward motions), and severe dizziness. It is, by the way, a known fact that alcohol inhibits the cerebellum, and this is why individuals who consume too much alcohol show signs of ataxia.

THE CEREBELLUM: THE CAPTAIN OF THE BODY'S COOPERATING ENERGY SYSTEM

The cerebellum is the second largest portion of the brain. It is behind the medulla and pons, and below the occipital lobes of the cerebrum, which is supported on the brain stem and forms the bulk of the brain. The cerebellum is a many folded structure concerned with equilibrium, muscle tone, and the coordination of voluntary muscle activity (i.e., synergy). Synergy literally means: combined action or operation, working together, cooperating in a system. When applied to the body then, it logically means a cooperating energy system that sets up conditions such that the total effect is greater than the sum of the individual effects. In other words, a body affected by problems in the cerebellum ends up wasting a lot of body motions inefficiently.

Unable to pull it all together, coordinate its efforts, the cerebellum is basically giving out garbled directions.

THE CEREBELLUM: SUPERINTENDENT OF THE BODY'S MOTOR BEHAVIORS

The cerebellum also exerts a very important influence on posture and movement, but does not exert this influence directly by pathways that descend to the motor neurons. Rather, the cerebellum affects motor behavior, by means of input to brain stem nuclei and by way of the thalamus to regions of the sensorimotor cortex. Motor behavior as defined in my dictionary is: 1.) Anything that an organism does involving action and response to stimulation as it pertains to muscular movement. Therefore, as I stated previously (and to be seen as an important distinction here) the cerebellum's role in motor functioning, at least in part; is to perform the critical task of comparing information about what the muscles should be doing, with information about what they actually are doing. Amazing part of the brain this cerebellum turns out to be, wouldn't you say? To achieve this, the cerebellum receives information both from the sensorimotor cortex (top of the brain relayed via brain-stem nuclei), the vestibular system, eyes, ears, skin, muscles, joints, tendons; that is, from the major receptors affected by movements.

CEREBELLUM: A PART OF OUR SUBCONSCIOUS BRAIN?

The cerebellum does this all without thinking, so to speak. Although the specialized neurons of the cerebellum have extensive dendrite branches, and can receive and process massive amounts of incoming information about the body's position and movement, their labors do not reach consciousness, so they are not able to "think" the way neurons in the cerebral cortex do. The cerebellum subconsciously refines and plans commands for muscle movements before they are

28

initiated by the cerebral cortex. The brain needs to know the position and speed of the body as a whole. It must know the position of each body limb. This is part of the body's memory. A discrepancy between the intended movement and the actual one, causes the cerebellum to send an __error signal__ to the motor cortex and subcortical centers to modify the central motor programs, correct the ongoing movement, and ensure that future movements of the same kind will be performed more accurately. **The cerebellum does all this without thinking.** In fact, the cerebellum plays an important role in the learning of motor skills, as it regulates the __timing__ of the complex muscle actions required for even the simplest motor act. This is all part of our amazing and wonderful human machine's memory that we take so much for granted each and every day. This wonderful body is working so hard all the time and we seldom say thank you, do we?

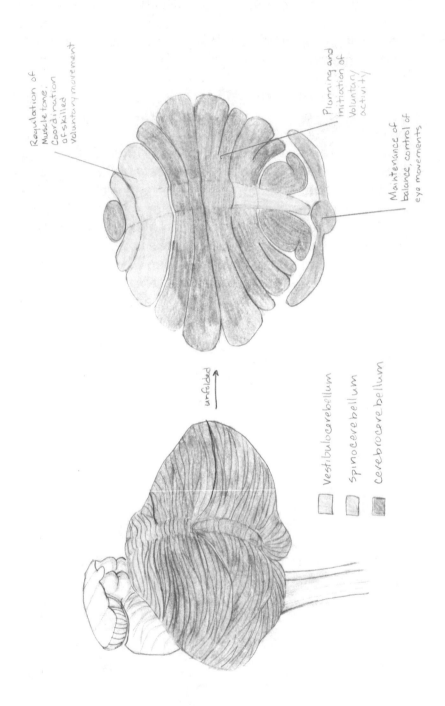

Regulation of Muscle tone. Coordination of skilled voluntary movement

Planning and initiation of voluntary activity

Maintenance of balance, control of eye movements

unfolded →

Vestibulocerebellum

Spinocerebellum

Cerebrocerebellum

BODY MEMORY: PRODUCED THROUGH NEURAL
SYSTEM CHANGE

This **body memory**, is another amazing feature of our nervous system as a whole. Memory is the ability to recall thoughts and experiences. For an experience to become part of our body memory, it <u>must</u> produce changes in the central nervous system that represent the experience. Such a memory trace in the nervous system, and particularly a specific area of the brain is called an engram, as it pertains to a neural change responsible for retention or storage of knowledge. Memory is the storage of acquired knowledge for later recall, and learning and memory form the basis by which individuals adapt their behavior to their particular external circumstances. This information from our external environment comes to our nervous system in a variety of ways. Some of this information comes through conscious visual pathways (sight) from the eyes to the occipital area of the cerebral cortex. These pathways <u>do not involve</u> the cerebellum, but they help us to see where we are.

THE EYE: ENABLES US TO SEE WHERE WE ARE IN
THE WORLD

The eye is like a camera. The eyes capture the patterns of illumination in the environment as an "optical picture" on a layer of light-sensitive cells, the retina, much like a camera captures an image on film. Just as film can be developed into a visual likeness of the original image, the coded image on the retina is transmitted though a series of progressively more complex steps of visual processing until it is finally consciously perceived as a visual likeness of the original image. The muscles of our eyes are controlled by our nervous system, and so it follows that due to muscle movement difficulty, children with cerebral palsy are more likely than other children to have certain vision problems. Half of all children with cerebral palsy have eye muscle imbalance or strabismus (crossed eyes) and refractive errors (nearsightedness or farsightedness). In strabismus, both eyes do not focus together. An eye can turn in, or out, but either problem can cause double vision and affect depth perception. Melissa's eyes were straightened or realigned as I stated previously, at fourteen months, but to this day I feel she has a great deal of difficulty with depth perception. Since the cerebellum is an elaborate integrating system, it stands to reason for me to believe, that a part of this muscle problem still prevails despite the surgery. As a part of ataxia, caused by damage to the cerebellum, movements become uncoordinated but also result in errors in direction, range, and rate of movement. In attempting to touch an object, an ataxic individual will overshoot first to one side and then to the other (called intention tremor). An individual with cerebellar damage specifically will miss the mark, and may miss the mark several times completely before finding the target.

In Melissa's case I feel her difficulty in feeding herself to this day is a result of this lack of depth perception, or inability to hit the target, namely her mouth. She feeds herself, and that is the important thing in my mind and hers, but basically the whole table looks like her plate at times. I tell her to concentrate on what she is doing, and bless her heart she tries so hard, but at her twenty five years of age it is difficult to watch your daughter unable to "hit her mouth" when eating. This focusing difficulty I still believe to be visual in origin. It is true that the motor problems of children with cerebral palsy can and do affect eye muscle control and cause the misalignment of the eyes, but the depth perception problem seems to persist, in my mind.

32

Sagittal Section of Brain and Spinal Cord

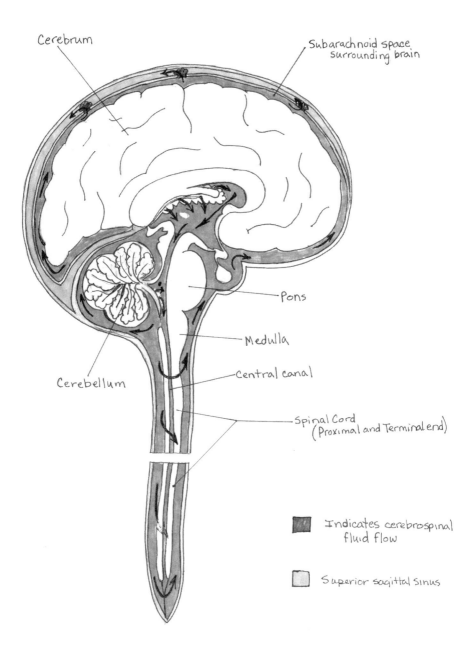

Cerebrum

Subarachnoid space surrounding brain

Pons

Medulla

Cerebellum

Central canal

Spinal Cord (Proximal and Terminal end)

Indicates cerebrospinal fluid flow

Superior sagittal sinus

THE CEREBELLUM: A SILENT AREA OF THE BRAIN

The cerebellum has long been called a **silent area of the brain**, principally because electrical excitation of this structure <u>does not</u> cause any sensation and rarely causes any motor movement. Removal of the cerebellum, however, <u>does cause movement to become highly abnormal</u>. The cerebellum is especially vital, we know, to the control of rapid muscular activities, such as running, typing, playing the piano, and even talking. Loss of this area of the brain can cause almost total incoordination of these activities even though its loss causes no paralysis of muscles.

THE CEREBELLUM LEARNS BY ITS MISTAKES

The most important aspect of the cerebellum I have been told by experts, is that the cerebellum apparently learns by its mistakes. Isn't that amazing? Learns by its mistakes!!! If a movement does not occur exactly as intended, the cerebellar circuit learns to make a stronger or weaker movement the next time. To do this, changes occur in the excitability of the appropriate cerebellar neurons, thus bringing the subsequent contractions of body movement into better correspondence with the intended movements. Is memory, body memory, somehow embedded in the cerebellum circuitry? Does that mean that my daughter was somehow lacking in muscle memory because her cerebellum had never grown or matured to the extent to think for her muscles? Those muscles couldn't remember because her cerebellum couldn't remember? If the cerebellum does continually collect information about the movements and positions of all parts of the body on a subconscious level, then a disorder of this type would or could be classified as a memory disorder of the cerebellum could it not? At a very young age could we have stimulated that muscle memory by stimulating those muscles?

BODY MEMORY: AN AMAZING FEATURE OF OUR NERVOUS SYSTEM

As I stated previously, body memory is an amazing feature of our nervous system, as a whole. Memory is the ability to recall thoughts, and experiences. The most important aspect of this body memory therefore is based on the fact that an experience **must** produce changes in the central nervous system that represent that given experience to become part of our body memory. For that reason, at eighteen months of age, we decided to act upon the recommendation given to us concerning the patterning of this body memory for Melissa. Fraser School became Melissa's school home for integration of this body pattern stimulation, or infant stimulation, as it was also called. Melissa left "me" home alone at the age of eighteen months.

I had intended to stay home with my baby daughter, who I had waited so long for and be the perfect mother. The boys were twelve and thirteen years of age, and I regretted the fact that I was not able to stay home with them when they were little. This was going to be my chance and here Melissa blew it for me by leaving me home and going off to school. She was so strong minded that she didn't cry, and I cried all day. She had to be supported by others in her pink snowsuit on the bus and here her healthy, strong-bodied mother was a "blubbering" bawl baby. I baked those precious cookies for my kids and ate most of them myself. It was consoling, like my pillow of "denial", "food" can also be comforting. I finally went back to work before I gained so much weight that I would break the chairs I sat in all day.

Melissa thrived at Fraser School, and loved being around the other children. She was at school from 9 a.m. to 3 p.m. during the day. There was a music room that Melissa especially enjoyed. The floor was insulated somehow so the deaf children could feel the music through their feet. Melissa, who would rock in rhythm to music in her crib as a baby, thought this was pretty special, which was obvious when I observed her there. She did not elaborate verbally on what she liked or did not like at that age, at home or school, but if you observed her, you knew. Her verbal communication was limited, as it is now, but what "You saw was what you got," if you paid attention to Melissa's body language.

There was speech therapy, physical therapy, some basic learning skills, e.g., colors and shapes, but mostly it was centered around "developing patterns, or grooves," in Melissa's young mind and brain, as far as we understood it. There was a distinct separation between school and home, and we did not fully understand the long-range concept of infant stimulation or patterning. We were told just to enjoy her at home, and I do not remember being taught the logistics of the method. Looking back, classes and training in the method would have been extremely helpful, but at that point in time I could not see the years spanning ahead of us living with the diagnosis of cerebral palsy, and what I would need to know over the years. I was concerned with arresting the disorder, as I still did not fully understand that cerebral palsy is a "non-progressive disability." The diagnosis was the most important thing in my mind. The diagnosis consumed so much of my energy, it's amazing I had anything left for the boys and my husband. Let me sleep in my pillow of "denial," and wake me when she's "well."

My boys were so good with Melissa right from the start. They thought she was a little doll, until the doll cried, and then it was time for mom to take over. She could sit with support, but had difficulty maintaining her balance, so those two boys had the patience of saints with this little doll that could not be wound up to sit, walk, or talk. She'd curl in between them on the floor and watch T.V. Somehow those two roughnecks were so gentle with her, she was **never** hurt. She loved those boys then, and now. To this day these grown men are her "idols." She'll

36

get out of her wheelchair, and crawl after the older brother especially. This thirty six year old man somehow captured her heart so completely as a young boy, he lives still within her mind, as someone who will **never** leave her out or treat her differently.

FRASER SCHOOL: WHAT A BLESSING FOR MELISSA MARIE AND ME!!

Fraser School made us aware of the importance of Melissa's balance. We were checking her balance by encouraging her to sit, and most of all use the walker to get up on her feet, and thereby increase her strength overall continually, and especially her legs. It was Fraser School that got her standing on those stubborn legs, and gave her the mobility that is still present today. Whatever she could do through the school's assessment was viewed by Fraser School as a strength, and whatever strength was found, she was encouraged to use. To this day she has very strong arms. She pulls herself up with those strong arms to a standing position to the amazement of many, above and beyond what is considered usually to be the result of either great ability or of much training in the non-handicapped population.

Perhaps this was due in part to our constant checking her "righting" reactions at an early age. The lack of, or distortion of **"righting"** reactions against gravity, is a strong clue to therapists to the presence of a neuromotor disorder. These "righting" reactions normally occur early in development, and since they provide one means of early identification of the infant who is in trouble, I've always felt my instinctive need to see if Melissa could hold herself up or right herself if I pushed gently on her, was actually a strengthening exercise for her upper torso. I am proud of her strength, and proud of my part in encouraging it for her, at a young age. This little doll that could not be wound up to sit, walk, or talk by others, by her self-determination winds herself up to do whatever she can do, each and every day of her life.

THE UNIQUE AND SPECIAL CEREBELLUM: THE PART OF MELISSA'S BRAIN THAT DID NOT GROW

The full truth of what had gone awry in Melissa's brain was that her cerebellum, or little brain, had simply never grown. As I stated earlier, the cerebellum has many special and unique characteristics and functions, but one amazing quality is the "control of coordination of the limbs on the same side of the body." "Everything in the brain except for the cerebellum is backward in that the right side of the brain controls the left side of the body." The cerebellum is composed of two hemispheres and a central portion, the "vermis." Essentially, each hemisphere controls motor coordination of the ipsilateral (same side) limbs, and the "vermis" (central portion) controls coordination of "midline structures," which are the head, neck, and trunk. Another unique feature of the cerebellum is that, when one hemisphere is damaged, the other will eventually be able to perform almost all the function for both. Thus, although loss of one cerebellar hemisphere will cause incapacitating dysfunction of the same sided limbs, most patients regain function of the affected limbs within one year. Also, although acute cerebellar lesions cause impaired coordination on the same side as the lesion, they do not cause paralysis or significant reflex abnormality. **Damage of the entire cerebellum, or the vermis (central portion), alone causes incoordination of the entire trunk of the body.**

Even more important, since the cerebellum is isolated from the cerebral hemispheres, or higher thinking areas, even **its total destruction does not cause intellectual abnormalities**. A good example of the lack of cognitive function in the cerebellum is the normal cognitive capacity of children who have undergone resection of a cerebellar hemisphere for treatment of trauma, or a cerebellar malignant tumor.

QUESTION: WAS MELISSA SMARTER THAN WE ALL GAVE HER CREDIT FOR?

So where did Melissa's "mental retardation diagnosis" originate in her brain, if not from her cerebellum? In one reference my nurse friend found, it said the intelligent child is able to attempt movement even when the effort results in abnormal patterns. Certainly Melissa's frog-like crawling pattern was abnormal, but the intelligent child will attempt it apparently, so was Melissa more intelligent than she was given credit for? She has never tested well with the professionals. Always under-performs, in my opinion, so she won't have to work as hard, I always thought. Was this an intelligent stance, even when she was young? Are underachievers smarter than the average bear in the opposite direction?

THEN SHE GOT SPACY! WHAT WILL HAPPEN NEXT?

One area of her disability that was not addressed, in my opinion, were her staring spells. They happened often when she was a baby, and up to about the age of five. The staring spells did not last for a long period of time, but they did happen. With Melissa's visual difficulties, I assumed these spells had a visual basis. There was a definite lack of adequate sustained head positioning in Melissa, which would allow her eyes to develop sustained focus and orientation to the environment, so I thought my little girl was "strengthening her own eye focus." Oh what a smart little baby I had. However, when someone mentioned it could be petit mal seizures to me, I was totally stunned. What next, I thought? I thought seizures were "Fall down, hit the floor, foam at the mouth kind of things." Oh my God, I thought, "What will happen next to my baby?"

I began to research petite mal seizures with my nurse friend. In her dictionary they were also called absence seizures. Can you believe it? Now she had a condition

40

that wasn't really there? Or did it mean she wasn't really there? Or would it mean she would progressively get more "out there." Absence seizures, I found out, were one to ten second lapses in attention, accompanied in almost all cases by automatisms (subtle clonic contractions and relaxations of muscles and limb movements), and blinking. Oh great, I thought, she's fading out, not in. She's not focusing, she's in the "ozone." I also found in my reading that children with unrecognized absences **may be misdiagnosed as being inattentive or mentally retarded.**

ABSENCE SEIZURES: A REAL THING.

In studying further I found that petit mal seizures are a real thing. They are manifested solely by repeated transient loss, or impairment, of consciousness. Attacks last only from five to thirty seconds, and may be scarcely noticeable to others. The victim, as though momentarily dazed, stops talking, walking, or whatever he or she is doing - then resumes, as though no interruption had occurred: To them the attack was just a blank moment. A rhythmic twitching of the eyelids or the head may be observed during the attack. They may jerk their heads or make some other automatic motion, sometimes a violent one, and then a sudden muscular collapse may allow the head to nod or the patient to crumple, suddenly helpless, to the ground. Whatever its manifestations, petit mal epilepsy is distinguished by its rarity in adults and by the frequency of its attacks, which may recur several times each day. Today they are called "childhood absence epilepsy," instead of "petit mal epilepsy," as the description fits those cases in which absence attacks are and remain the only seizure type, as Melissa's did. Her absence attacks started in early childhood and consisted only of brief losses of consciousness that lasted a few seconds, As mysteriously as they began, just as mysteriously they stopped. She had a dazed appearance, the eyes did stare, but she never fell or had a full convulsion. As soon as the attack has passed, these individuals go on as if nothing had happened, as Melissa did. In some cases the individual may not even be completely unconscious. Some do have a feeling that something is not quite right and can describe the state of abnormality as more of an odd sensation rather than something they can put their finger on or describe exactly. What Melissa thought or felt was a mystery to me then and will remain a mystery forever, I am sure. The question remains in my mind and I have often wondered, if these "absences" were somehow responsible for her label of mental retardation?

FRIEND NURSE'S LECTURE: MENTAL RETARDATION, HOW DO WE KNOW FOR SURE?

"Unable to talk with infants, developmental researchers have assessed what they can observe about infants to ascertain their intellectual capacity. Everything from birth weight to head circumference, to whether the third toe was longer than the second, to the age of sitting up alone." (Psychology, 3rd Edition, David G. Myers.) However, none of these measures provide any useful prediction of intelligence scores at much later ages. (Bell & Waldrop, 1989: Broman, 1989.)

To be labeled mentally retarded, a child must have both a low intelligence test score (below 70) and have difficulty adapting to the normal demands of life. This difficulty adapting to the normal demands of life must then subsequently lead to the inability of living independently. Only about 1% of the population meets both of these criteria, with males outnumbering females by 50%. (American Psychiatric Association, 1987.)

There is much debate about the causes of mental retardation, as often there is no tangible evidence of organic brain damage that can be detected. However, there are innumerable causes of retardation for a certain percent of the below 70 IQ group who have recognizable pathological conditions. Some of them include: 1.) chromosomal anomalies, 2.) abnormalities of gestation, 3.) maternal dietary deficiencies, 4.) metabolic disorders, 5.) virus infections of the mother and newborn, 6.) blood-type incompatibility, 7.) poisoning of the fetus due to lead, 8.) carbon monoxide, 9.) drugs and other substances ingested by the mother. (Heber, 1970.)

In past years it was thought that most cases of brain damage resulted primarily from birth injuries, but Masland (1958) concluded that the predisposing problem is **more likely** to have arisen early in the gestation period, primarily by the end of the third month of pregnancy.

43

The resulting fetus, being abnormal, produces an abnormal pregnancy which results in birth difficulties. Therefore, no longer are anoxia at birth, prematurity, and instrument births assumed to be the **major causes** of retardation. (Dunn, 1973.)

We do know, however, that impairments that involve the nervous system generally handicap the individual intellectually and educationally, more than other types of nonsensory physical disabilities or chronic health conditions. **Since the nervous system is the activating mechanism of the total body, none of the body's systems function without adequate performance of the nervous system. The capability of the central nervous system to react to environmental influences; to receive and conduct nerve impulses; to interpret, store, integrate, and process information; and to activate responses is essential in the learning process.**

Children, therefore, with neuromotor disabilities, often have impairment of learning ability, along with impairment of physical functioning. It is for this reason that children with neurological involvement, present one of the most complicated problems to the educational system as a learner.

CEREBRAL PALSY: NOT A DISEASE IN THE USUAL SENSE

Cerebral palsy is an impairment of the nervous system that cannot be considered a disease in the usual sense. The term designates a number of types of neuromuscular disabilities characterized by disturbances of motor function resulting from damage to the brain and central nervous system. Most children with cerebral palsy have other multiple handicapping conditions such as speech impairment and mental retardation, visual and

44

auditory impairment are also common. Taylor (1961) estimated that approximately half of the children with cerebral palsy are mentally retarded, with IQ scores below 70. The particular kinds of secondary defects, or handicaps, of course, would depend largely on the site, cause, and extent of damage to the brain. Since the damage areas of the brain cannot be repaired or replaced, treatment and education must begin with and be aimed at the symptoms rather than the cause, or to put it more succinctly: **What are the presenting symptoms at this time? This will lead you to where the child is, the needs, and where to go from there** with the care plan.

Cerebral palsy is motor incoordination, due to brain injury. It stands to reason that brain damage severe enough to result in readily discernible motor dysfunction can also result in intellectual inadequacy. Similarly, many cases of pathological retardation can, and are, labeled cerebral palsy arbitrarily. The label can be, and is often, a confusing one as it was for us with Melissa Marie. Brain injury can result from a large number of factors, but many very different types of central nervous system damage may occur. **In most cases the injury is diffused and general,** but in some cases a specific area of the brain may be particularly more damaged than another. With Melissa Marie, we knew at the age of twelve years that her cerebellum had not grown, but we really did not know and still do not know of further areas of involvement.

HOW DOES A MENTALLY RETARDED CHILD BEHAVE?

The behavioral characteristics of children with brain damage vary greatly. **Depending on the area and extent of the brain which has been damaged, these children may be hypoactive (lethargic), hyperactive (hyperkinetic),** or normal in activity

45

level. It is impossible to talk about brain injured children as a homogeneous group.

While most children with mild learning disabilities have few obvious physical and psychological disabilities, a large number of the moderately retarded, and even more of the severely retarded, demonstrate such signs at an early age. The vast majority of the moderate to severely retarded are identified at birth, or during their preschool years. In most cases the children lack coordination and exhibit a slowness in learning to sit, walk, and talk.

By late in the child's first year, or shortly thereafter, the suspicions and concerns of the family are aroused, and then the family physician is involved. However, since the family doctor is seldom an authority on retardation, the family is often referred to a professional clinic for diagnosis and evaluation. This diagnosis involves psychologists, social workers, physicians trained to evaluate such children, and other child care specialists. **These professionals can, and should, note how these children's perception and understanding of their environment, their reaction to those about them, and their adaptive responses to the attitudes and behavior of others may be quite different from those of a normal child at that age.**

A consideration of the adjustment problems of the mentally retarded child begins with the recognition that mental retardation may have a profound effect on the functioning of the individual in any, and all situations, but **the child will still function as a unitary whole. This concept needs constant emphasis in arriving at an understanding of the total functioning level of an individual mentally retarded child.**

ALL CHILDREN FUNCTION AS A UNITARY WHOLE

All human beings live and behave only as whole persons, therefore all aspects of their development are intimately connected. When we try to separate these aspects, we find ourselves making arbitrary divisions cutting the person into jigsaw pieces. For example, although we usually think of learning as a mental function, infants learn a great deal by action. Newborns cannot tell themselves apart from their surroundings until they begin to explore their environment, and learn from their own movements where their bodies end and the rest of the world begins. The brain itself is a physical organ, and such aspects of the brain's individual intelligence, learning, and personality, are inextricably linked with the physical aspects of the individual growth and development of the individual child, whether labeled mentally retarded or given the stamp of approval of "normal."

We do know, however, that babies usually do not have to be taught the basic motor skills: they just need freedom from interference. As soon as their central nervous systems, muscles, and bones are mature enough, they need only room and freedom to move, in order to keep showing surprising new abilities. They are persistent too. As soon as they acquire a new skill, they keep practicing and improving it. Each newly mastered skill prepares a child to tackle the next one in the sequence, and it is this proliferation of motor skills that gives the infant the increasing opportunity to explore and manipulate the environment and to experience sensory and cognitive stimulation.

Learning is a change in behavior that results from experience. Since cerebral palsy is not a progressive disorder, children with cerebral palsy can and do learn from experience, once they have experienced it. In other words, children with cerebral palsy do not stop activities once they have begun them; therefore, a loss of skills once they have attained them, is not characteristic of a child with cerebral palsy. If such a loss of acquired skills occurs, which is called regression, this loss of skill power is not characteristic of cerebral palsy.

It is important to keep in mind that each baby, each individual develops in his or her own way. The growth and development of infants with handicaps or chronic illnesses may be erratic in some areas, and showing some aspects of normal patterns of development in others. It is important, I believe, in this context, for parents to view development as a continuous process, rather than a series of milestones. Developmental "norms" are not absolutes. All children are individuals, and as such may gain individual skills earlier or later than other children. In other words, **"If compared to themselves, how normal is my child?"** When I learned to compare **Melissa Marie** only to **Melissa Marie...all of our lives** got **a lot easier.**

WHAT MELISSA MARIE'S MENTAL RETARDATION LABEL MEANT TO US

When we were given the verdict of her life-long sentence of mental retardation, I could almost hear and feel the steel doors closing on me and essentially around our whole family. The label of mental retardation is like the isolation of solitary confinement, in my mind. From that moment on, it was never again a consideration of what our beautiful little girl "could do" but what she "could not do." Everything turned into an arena of <u>achievement disability</u> testing for Melissa. Comments were directed at me as to having a false sense of hope for her. "Give it up!" "Learn to live with it!" "Don't expect too much, after all, she is mentally retarded!"

Instead of being like the little red engine of hope that said to itself, "I think I can, I think I can," eventually culminating at the top of the hill with, "I know I can, I know I can," we were continually faced with the uphill battle of hearing , "She can't, she can't, she can't!" Lost to us was the dream of hope for our child that most parents feel and need to feel. I kept thinking to myself, "But what if she can, and we don't give her an opportunity to even try to see what she can do?" I did learn that there are no maybes in mental retardation. There are no dreams. There are few hopes. There is just an overwhelming sense of loss and grief that goes with the diagnosis. It is like solid steel bars holding you confined and tied to the diagnosis, as if it were an impending death that will most assuredly be slow and painful. You wake up every morning expecting "It" all to have been a bad dream. "A nightmare," as my husband said so frequently, "from which we will awake!" Somehow though, this bad dream had no ending only the beginning - which was the diagnosis itself. All of life seemed to start from the day of the diagnosis. **The label, the label.**

THE LABEL OF MENTAL RETARDATION

All of life seems to hinge on the stigma, the pity, that others, who still have their hopes and dreams for their children and their own lives, lay at your door. Pity that leaves you isolated and alone, rather than comfort that envelops you and holds you in its arms. Pity in my dictionary means, "The tender or sometimes slightly contemptuous sorrow for one in misery or distress." When I read that, I could finally understand why **pity** is such an awful word in my mind. **Sympathy,** doesn't rate much higher for me when I looked up the word. It states, "Having common feelings." I felt I had no commonality with any of my former friends or even family. I saw friends who could no longer associate with us because they couldn't handle the pain they felt when they looked at Melissa and our family. Relatives who were at a loss to understand our grief, so they talked over **It,** around **It,** through **It,** while we had to stand, as if riveted to them, while they talked to us about our situation without really hearing what we were saying in return. It is amazing how suddenly you're carrying on a conversation with someone as if that, too, is a dream. You're alone with your problem in the middle of a crowd, alone with a growing sense of somehow becoming different yourself also - just because your child is **Different.**

Parenting a "Different" child does make you different. Parenting a "Different" child makes you look at everything differently. Parenting a "Different" child makes your whole world slow down to slow motion. You become an expert at seeing the look in other's eyes. You become an expert in observing the whole world for tell-tale signs of judging. Having a handicapped, "Different," child becomes a matter of blame, of fault. As if a handicapped child is a punishment, a fated decreed occurrence that you somehow deserved and got, and others feel above you and better than you for having escaped your prison of loss and pain.

My nurse friend calls it the "shunning syndrome." To shun means in my dictionary: 1.) to avoid deliberately and especially habitually, 2.) to keep clear of; to avoid consistently, 3.) to keep away from. That did sum up how I felt, especially being the mother. As Melissa Marie's mother, I was somehow more responsible for her disability. It was my problem. Isn't "It" always the mother's problem, regardless of which member of the family is affected? The "mother" goes to the doctor, the mother diagnoses for the doctor; the doctor depends on the mother to inform the doctor. **The mother, the mother, the mother.** How I wished I could be the **father** for just one minute. I never have been able to understand how men can always manage to avoid the real issue, the real point, in any dilemma. Women get themselves so involved in the multiplicity of all the points, that is true, and men usually miss the real point. I guess in retrospect **we were two pointless, clueless people, trying to find the common denominator to our problem, which, of course, was Melissa...but it took years to stop worrying about everyone and everything, but her.**

WORRY, WORRY, WORRY, POINTLESS WORRY

I worried about what others thought of me. I worried about what others thought of Melissa. I worried about what I should say in answer to the endless inquisitions I was subjected to about my child, my life, how I was handling it all. A simple, "How are you doing?," sent me off on a pointless tangent of verbal explanation of every facet of our lives. I told people things that they didn't want to hear - first of all and had little real interest in hearing in the second place, and, basically was none of their business hearing in the third place. Hardest of all, I told people who did not care enough to comfort me with an empathetic relating to what I was saying. They did not care enough about me, about Melissa, about cerebral palsy, and certainly did not care to hear about mental retardation. Why did I open up my heart and pour out my feelings to anyone who asked? Why did I have this need to talk, talk, and talk? Is that whole scenario a part of the denial process of loss? Do we verbalize our shock (when we finally can), over and over again to try to wake ourselves up to reality? Are we like stuck records, where our needles can't get past a certain groove until something, someone, some force, picks us up or pushes us onto the next groove?

Louise Whittebeck Fraser School was that first powerful force that moved us confidently to the next groove. For Melissa, four good, constructive, comfortable years, gave her and all of us, the strength to move into the public school system. At Fraser School the climate in the classrooms, and the whole school, actually, was cheerful, upbeat, lots of windows with light streaming in. It just plain had a feeling of warmth - the building and the personnel. I knew I wanted Melissa there. It was the first place that I felt hope. It was also the first place that I heard and began to understand the word: **empathy.** Empathy, in my dictionary is: 1.) the imaginative projection of a subjective state into an object, so that the object appears to be infused with it. What in the world did that mean I wondered? My nurse friend said, "To me it has always been like being able to see into an emotion or person through your eyes, but you're not really inside the person or living the emotion, but you do have an idea of how they're feeling without having the feeling youself." Or as the second definition states in my dictionary: 1.) the action of understanding, being aware of, being sensitive to, and vicariously experiencing the feelings, thoughts, and experience communicated in an objective explicit manner. Well, I thought, the whole thing just plain sounded like, "It's knowing how it would feel to walk in my shoes, without actually being in them, actually entering into the feelings or experiences of another person or object, but not feeling the actual experience so you can stand back and understand what is going on in their lives more clearly, and be of more assistance to them."

52

To put it more simply, Fraser School understood Melissa and her needs and understood her family and the family's needs. I sorely missed that understanding when we entered into the public school system. I knew it would be a different world. I just didn't know how different! Melissa, who never handled change well, as is true of all handicapped children, in my experience, had difficulty adapting to a new school in the first place, and then she was transferred to a different school and different district three years in a row. She became totally confused as to where and how she fit into the scheme of things. It took months for the teacher to get to know and understand her needs and by that time we were on to a new school. The changes were never explained to my husband or I, and so we were as much in the dark as Melissa. As confused as we were, imagine what this was like in her "little world."

Empathy was an unheard of word, as no-one seemed to understand what was to be accomplished for Melissa. We would go to the meetings and do the IEP's, which sounded good while the professionals were talking, but we'd get home and wonder, "What did we really accomplish for Melissa?" I had the biggest problem with the fact that my little girl was in school, but she was not sitting at a desk. No academic surroundings, or at least none that I recognized. "You're old-fashioned," my husband would say to me. Maybe I was, but if my child was smart enough to be in school, then I thought she should be in school to learn, not just taking up floor space.

My continuous questioning as to what Melissa was learning irritated more than one educational professional. After all, my child was being mainstreamed, I was told, but it seemed to me that eating lunch with the rest of the school was a far cry from my idea of how mainstreaming had been explained to me. Regardless of my thoughts concerning what Melissa did or did not learn, my biggest concern for her was not being in a desk for posture reasons. My daughter, who had always needed support to her back, needed to be in a supportive position certainly for some hours of the long day. At home, if she wasn't in a chair, she would lay on her abdomen at intervals to rest her back. I remember most vividly all the rounded little backs. "Children, who I was sure would suffer with back pain or chest pain in their adult years?" I remember little rounded backs, sitting in a circle, playing the game, "Gray Duck, Gray Duck." Sort of like, The Farmer in the Dell, from my vintage days. What was the purpose of this game for Melissa though, I could not help but wonder? Some could run when they were the "gray duck" but Melissa had to crawl, and so I thought, more than once, that the purpose of the game was more to keep "me" busy sewing patches on the knees of her pants. At least they were doing something with my child, and so I should be satisfied with the physical aspect of her progress, and hopefully not keep inquiring about the learning aspect of her school progress. The game did not seem to have an academic purpose to me, but then it only lasted through the first, second and third grades, and so at least there was an end to the game, and my worry about the game.

The schools did not have the special education children placed in a grade sequence, and so Melissa wasn't ever in a specific grade, so to speak. **She was in Special Ed.** I had difficulty when someone would ask me what grade Melissa was in now? "What is she learning in Special Ed?," inquisitive people would ask. "She's in Special Ed," I would answer. What is she learning in Special Ed," inquisitive people would ask? "Well," I would say, "she certainly is learning the words gray duck, and I am learning how to sew on patches faster and faster every day. Add to that, I'm also too busy to be asking foolish questions like, "What is my daughter learning in school?"

THEN CAME SURGERY ON MELISSA'S ANKLES: A BLESSING IN DISGUISE

After being bounced around the public school system for three years, Melissa had to have corrective surgery on her ankles. This was a necessary procedure to be done at this time, as she was actually walking on the side of her feet. They were so turned over, she was walking on the inside of her ankle bone with her walker. Surgery was done by removing a bone from the shin area on both legs, and the bone fused to the ankle, forcing the foot to be maintained in a straight position. Spikes were then driven up through the heel to hold everything in place while her legs healed, and then removed six months later. Full length casts (one for each leg), going from hips to toes were applied, and immobilized Melissa completely for one month. The casts were then changed to below the knees on both legs.

She went to sleep with bare legs in the a.m. in the hospital, and woke up in the p.m. with these "monsters" on her legs. She simply could not comprehend what was going to happen before surgery, and certainly did not comprehend what was going on when she woke up. "Take off Mom, take off Mom, " were her first words. At eight years of chronological age, and less than that of mental age, there was no way of getting through to her mind the necessity of those "plaster monsters." When she had exhausted all of her efforts to have me remove them, then she began to tell me to "cover them Mom." Always a visually oriented child from babyhood on, "out of sight, was out of mind," for Melissa. When she was not able to orient herself to her surroundings by sight, she would then resort to sound. It would be, "Hi Mom, Hi Mom, Hi Mom," until I would finally in exasperation say, "Sorry Melissa, I just changed my name to Dad." She would smile, and say once again, "Hi Mom."

So here we were stuck together like glue, but with plaster of Paris for the cement. Bless her heart, she really didn't complain much. Her dad meanwhile, fell off a truck and fractured his heel about a month later. He was laid up for six months, and so was Melissa. I heard a lot of, "Hi Mom," "Where you at Mom?," and, "More pillows Honey!"

A NEW SCHOOL EXPERIENCE

With the now even more specialized needs for her care, the public school that was available in our area was Michael Dowling. Melissa needed to be carried and lifted everywhere, with her double casts on both legs. She was able to sit in the wheelchair when placed there, but certainly had lost all independent mobility, and had to learn to request all her bodily needs to be met. I, who had even learned to understand her grunts over the years, found that this rapport she had with me was not so easily attained with Melissa and the outside world. She simply was not that verbally expressive, and still is not with everyone, and even the speech pathologist at Michael Dowling would become frustrated with her lack of verbal expression.

This aspect of her total disability, which is in part her communication pattern, has followed through all of her life up to now. On every IEP (Individual Education Plan) there has always been one goal that specified: Melissa will ask for assistance. Melissa will ask for help when needed. Well, I'm sorry, Melissa never asked for much of anything, including help. At an early age Melissa just looked at what she wanted, and I learned to follow her gaze and see what she was saying with her eyes. She was so visually oriented, she used her eyes instead of her mouth, and anyone who paid any attention whatsoever to her body language, could read her like Braille. To this day if she wants her second serving of pie, which I usually carefully hide in the oven, she will stare at the oven door until I ask her what she wants, and she just continues staring a little bit harder like, "Read my eyes, Mom!"

A VISUAL LEARNER:
INFORMATION REWRITTEN FROM
DR. WALTER B. BARBE'S BOOK:
"GROWING UP LEARNING: THE KEY TO YOUR
CHILD'S POTENTIAL"

Visual, as the meaning relates to the sense of sight, means producing a visual memory of a scene, reproducing an image of what is seen, in the mind. To the visual learner the world is a series of pictures they are photographing and then viewing and reviewing from the album in their mind.

"Seeing is believing," for the visual learner. In that respect they are very sensitive to facial expressions, and moods manifested through body language expressed by those around them. Their processing pattern of sensory information is one of clarifying what is seen and observed over a period of time into a perceptual translation of their environment. Visual learners have to see their thoughts in their mind before being able to verbally or kinesthetically express them. This process takes time, as in any photo development, and often the visual learner will appear to be daydreaming or not paying attention while they are actually busy processing information in their mind.

Everything has to be in place for the visual learner, as structure is extremely important to them. They are meticulous about detail, and often become impatient when they are not able to recreate in words or writing what they see in their mind. Visual learners tend to be introverted, as they think in pictures, visualize in detail, and enjoy alone time for their vivid visual imaginations to occupy their minds. This alone time gives them the opportunity to put their thoughts and feelings into their own pictures to be expressed and then communicated when they are ready.

If you are not a visual learner, or have had little or no dealings or experience with a visual learner, you may have difficulty communicating with a visual learner or understanding a visual learner at first. A visual learner tends to be quiet and reserved, and holds back on expressing his or her mind. Their halting way of speaking at times causes them to use words clumsily when describing something new or to be searching for the word they haven't yet "seen" pop up on their own private "video screen." Visual learners have to "see" something clearly in their mind's eye before being able to organize their thoughts on paper, or verbally, in a comfortable manner. They are deliberate thinkers, planning things out well in advance, drawing comparisons, and noticing similarities and differences in the components of a new concept they are learning. Like "J.B. Fletcher," they don't miss much but can irritate those around them greatly with their keen powers of observation and the ability to focus on details that often others do not see.

Your visual learner is a "watcher." They are very careful to watch what is going on in an activity before participating. They are not going to be the first one to volunteer for demonstrating a new activity. Their best way of learning and participating is to observe or have an activity demonstrated to them so they can better grasp the concept of what they are to do or say.

A visual learner would be more apt to remember the color, appearance, and style of your clothes than your name. A visual learner visualizes what they are to learn before they put the process to work in their lives. Because of this all pervasive pattern of slower and more meticulous information processing, the visual learner can appear overall "slower" at times in their learning process to those who do not understand the visual learner's communication style.

As we know, children's far vision develops before their near vision. Visual learners, hanging on to this innate tendency of space in their visual mind, often "see" the results ahead of time, before the work is "done." In other words, the visual child can give up before trying because the picture is completed in their mind too early. The visual child is unable to explain their lack of motivation to try or to explain what they are thinking and why they are not working. Usually this slow deliberate processing pattern has "seen" the results of efforts before the efforts have even begun. In their mind's eye, then, there is no need to process further or expend energy needlessly.

This slow information processing pattern may also result in a child not speaking as early or with as much clarity as some children do. Adults may see the visual learner as being slow, with a speech impairment or communication delay, when this is actually not the case. Visual learners need to be drawn into participation with much encouragement to share their thoughts and pictures in their minds. They need patient mentors and teachers who will allow them the time and space to develop their pictures, as all professional photographers need. They also require time for retakes, touching up, and analyzing their results, as all professional photographers need. They also need and want company with them as they attend their private picture show, but company that will encourage, rather than discourage, what their private home movies are showing.

Books will be life long friends to the visual learner. Reading gives them the opportunity for thoughtful activity full of images and with their vivid imaginations can enable them to see more of life in full color. Their visual sensory system has a high tech button for acuity it seems. This sharpness of vision, this keen sense of visual perception they are apparently born with, enables them to perceive their world best and most efficiently through what they "see." The visual learner insists that others look at everything they are talking about and will use words such as, "Do you see?", meaning actually, "Do you understand?" Seeing is understanding to the visual learner... as the visual learner constantly attempts to clarify and understand their world through what they see!!!

MICHAEL DOWLING: A REAL SCHOOL LEARNING EXPERIENCE

Michael Dowling became a real school learning experience for Melissa. In that respect her surgery may have been a blessing in disguise. Her legs got fixed, and also her mind got worked on. Her first teacher at Michael Dowling worked wonders with Melissa. She never expected Melissa to tell her what she needed, or knew, or wanted. She always said, "Show me Melissa," or, "Let me see what you can do Melissa." It was the most amazing experience to watch Melissa unfold for this intuitive, visually oriented teacher. Looking back now I can see how starved Melissa was for a teacher that could look into her mind without having to be told where to look, or asked to look. A teacher who just knew where her ON switch was. Melissa reacted, responded to this teacher like "a little computer," which was the teacher's analogy. She said, "Once Melissa got it, you couldn't feed it into her fast enough." Like a hungry child, starved for information, her mind was set in motion by this teacher. The ON switch appeared to be located nearer her visual center, it seemed to me, as it was visual stimulation that seemed to set her in motion. Words and actions had very little effect, then or now. Visual stimulation was like the spigot regulating the flow of Melissa's thinking process. The flow of her information processing system somehow seemed to begin visually when the spigot was opened.

She would lay in bed and practice her spelling words over and over, until often I would say, "It's time to go to sleep now Melissa." Always saying the word first and then spelling them letter by letter, as if some magical marker in her mind was setting the word forth for her. I had told her to write her words in the air, and perhaps that is what she was doing. Sometimes she would have the list in front of her, but more often than not she appeared to be reading them in the air. Maybe I should have been a teacher, like I should have been a doctor?

Melissa became so proficient at spelling, she actually came in second place in a classroom spelling bee. The word that put her in second place instead of first place was, "school." Her spelling of the word was "scool," and about this time it was on the news that the President of the United States had also misspelled the word "school." We jokingly told Melissa that she was at least in good company with that spelling error.

Those good, fun years of learning lasted four years for Melissa. She was happy, and so was I. Then at the age of 12 she was too old for Michael Dowling and had to return to the regular public school system. As before, this was a difficult transition for her, and her parents. She actually went through a six week time of depression. A close neighbor had passed away, also, at this time, and it seemed to be an accumulation of losses for Melissa. She would just lay and cry, which was not Melissa. She didn't want to go to school and would just repeat, and repeat, and repeat, "No school Mom." The interesting part of this scene was that only for me did she put on this visual display of a totally despondent human being. For everyone else, including her father, she was the same old Melissa, happy-go-lucky. Everyone was beginning to think I had a problem and then finally this kind, intuitive psychologist in private practice came to our house one day at my request. In one session with Melissa in our back yard, the depression was lifted. I have no idea what transpired between them and did not ask, did not care to know. Some situations are just better left in the hands of a "knowing" professional.

THE SOCIAL CHALLENGES WITH A HANDICAPPED CHILD

We were warned by a social worker, early on, to be prepared to encourage Melissa in social contacts and social outlets. In that regard she was a Brownie and then a Girl Scout while at Michael Dowling, and now, at twenty five years of age, she is a Girl Scout alumni. There are meetings monthly, and work towards achieving badges for recognition of accomplished tasks. Over Memorial Day each year Melissa attends a three day Girl Scout camp, which she thoroughly enjoys. We are so lucky to have a most kind and generous lady by the name of Eloise, who gives her all to our special young lady. Believe me, we enjoy our Memorial Day weekend off by ourselves.

At the present time she belongs to a group called "Happenings," which is provided through a local park board. They do a variety of activities which have included: bowling, movies, Valley Fair, dinner, and even wheelchair dancing. Melissa loves to be involved in activities which include mixed company. I have always felt that her positive relationship with her brothers and her dad have a great deal to do with her feelings toward the opposite sex. This can be a worry at times. In every form I fill out for camp or anything else, it is necessary to make them aware of the fact that she is a vulnerable adult with the opposite sex.

Another group, from which she gains much support and encouragement is "Faith and Light." It is an international ecumenical association for mentally handicapped people, their families and friends. Activities include meetings, social affairs, which always include meals for the handicapped and families, and fund raisers which enable the handicapped individuals to: 1.) attend Camp Confidence located in Brainerd, Minnesota, and 2.) some individuals have even flown to other conference sites through the efforts of the fund raisers.

The meetings of thirty or more handicapped individuals of any age is not like a regular meeting as you would envision it. This is not to say it is chaos but it can get a little hectic with more than one person with lack of impulse control in the room. Regardless of the effort involved for the parents, it is a most rewarding experience for all of us, and a continual learning experience in social exchange for all the handicapped individuals.

The warning given to us by the intuitive social worker early on was a most prudent one as it alerted us to the realization, even before it hit us, that in high school and after there is little in the way of social functions the handicapped can be involved in.

HIGH SCHOOL FOR MELISSA: BASIC TRAINING IN WORK SKILLS

Special education for a high school student was comprised basically of learning a variety of job skills and daily living independent skills. The job Melissa loved was folding boxes for Pizza Hut. She would be transported, in the beginning, with an aide and eventually was transported by Metro Mobility, a transportation service for the handicapped, on her own. The job she hated most was laundry. She had to fold aprons, shirt jackets, etc., and in retrospect, I believe her posture disabilities had a profound effect on her inability to do the job well and comfortably. Basically always a perfectionist, whatever she did she put 100% into it and if she couldn't do a job well she had difficulty articulating why she was having trouble. She would say matter of factly, "I hate laundry." At home she always would fold her own laundry, and seemed to enjoy doing it, but of course they are smaller items and did not give her the same difficulty the larger items gave her, with her persistent posture, reaching, and stretching problems. Standing, reaching, changing posture positions were a matter of balance stability problems for Melissa and continue to be so until the present time. We're right back to that cerebellum that never grew, aren't we?

THE CEREBELLUM: A RATHER HOMELY AND ISOLATED ORGAN, BUT OH, WHAT A NECESSARY ORGAN FOR FLUID MOTOR MOVEMENT

By now you have surely realized how thankful I am each and every day for my healthy cerebellum. As a whole, the cerebellum is a rather homely and isolated organ. It is attached to the back of the upper portion of the brain stem, and lies underneath the occipital lobe of the cortex. The cerebellum is organized into an outer layer of gray matter with white matter underneath. The cerebellum's treelike arrangement of white matter is called the "arbor vitae" (meaning the tree of life). The cerebellum's outside cortex of gray matter is home for millions of neurons. **Purkinje cells,** the specialized neurons of the cerebellar cortex, have extensive dendrite branches. They can receive and process massive amounts of incoming information about the body's position and movement. Although the neurons of the cerebellum are always at work, I repeat, they do not "think" the way neurons in the cerebral cortex do. However, without the cerebellum, we could never keep on our toes or walk a straight line. For the athlete, ballet star, and steel worker alike, it is the cerebellum that balances, smoothes out technique, and coordinates the limbs to create the "right moves." In other words, before the cerebral cortex can execute the right moves, the cerebellum **must** first define exactly what right will mean. Only then can the actions of the opposing muscles blend into one **fluid motion,** in the desired direction, at the desired time.

So how is it that the cerebellum can be so important when it has no direct ability to cause muscle contraction? The answer is that it helps to sequence the motor activities and also monitors and makes corrective adjustments in the body's motor activities so that they will conform to the motor signals directed by the motor cortex and other parts of the brain. This sequencing of motor activities through our musculoskeletal system allows the body to maintain a homeostasis, or balance, between systems of that body. The musculoskeletal system moves us to where we want to go, and need to go - to eat, to work, to play, to flee from danger. Our brain is the "Big Cheese," that makes all of it possible. The cerebellum is the second largest part of that "Big Cheese," the brain, the master control system of the human body.

One of the most important output pathways of the cerebellum is to the red nucleus of the midbrain, which relays information from the cerebellum to the spinal cord. In this way it functions indirectly by modifying the output of major motor systems of the brain. The spinal cord is responsible for the integration of many basic reflexes. **A reflex is any response that occurs automatically without conscious effort.** The spinal cord is strategically located between the brain and to and fro fibers of the peripheral nervous system, so that it may fulfill its two primary functions:

1. serving as a link for transmission of information between the brain and the remainder of the body,
2. integrating reflex activity between input (afferent) and output (efferent) impulses without involving the brain.

This is known as the spinal reflex, in other words, "Let the Big Cheese sleep. Well, we know the brain essentially never sleeps completely, but it does sometimes rest or go on automatic control.

AUTONOMIC SYSTEM/SUBCONSCIOUS LEVEL OF NERVOUS SYSTEM FUNCTIONING

A large segment of the nervous system is called the **autonomic system.** It operates at a subconscious level and controls many functions of the internal organs, including the level of pumping activity by the heart, movements of the gastrointestinal tract, and glandular secretion. The nervous system is composed of three major parts:

1. The sensory input portion
2. The central nervous system (integrative portion)
3. The motor output portion

Sensory receptors detect the state of the body or the state of the surroundings. For instance, receptors present everywhere in the skin appraise you every time an object touches the skin at any point. The eyes are sensory organs that give one a visual image of the surrounding area. The ears also are sensory organs. The brain can store information, generate thought, create ambition, and determine reactions the body performs in response to the sensations. Appropriate signals are then transmitted through the motor output portion of the nervous system to carry out one's wishes. We know that the various parts of the nervous system receive and analyze the messages and decide automatically what should be done. When some action is needed in a hurry, the "order," perhaps to contract a muscle, is telegraphed back to the part of the body involved. The signal or impulse then travels out to the muscle fibers in the area where the impulse started. The impulse triggers the muscle fibers and causes them to contract.

A nerve impulse can travel along a human nerve fiber at a speed of about 100 yards a second, or nearly 200 miles an hour. In moving through the network or nerve fibers, the impulse travels by a sort of chain reaction. In cerebral palsy then, I can't help but think that the impulse or memory must be lost somewhere in this chain of events. Makes sense to me anyway. Rather like a short circuit somewhere in the chain of events and since Melissa seems to short circuit a lot, that was how I looked at it.

THE INTEGRATIVE FUNCTION OF THE BODY'S NERVOUS SYSTEM

The most important ultimate role of the nervous system is to control the various bodily activities. This is achieved by controlling:

1. contraction of skeletal muscles throughout the body
2. contraction of smooth muscle in the internal organs
3. secretion by both exocrine and endocrine glands in many parts of the body.

These activities are collectively called "motor functions" of the nervous system, and the muscles and glands are called "effectors" because they perform the functions dictated by the nerve signals. **In other words, the major function of the nervous system is to process incoming information in such a way that appropriate motor responses occur.** It is documented that the cerebellum cannot initiate muscle function by itself and it must always function in association with other systems of motor control. It appears then that cerebral palsy is a condition of lack of coordination with other parts of the nervous system, certainly as far as Melissa and her undeveloped cerebellum are concerned.

The cerebellum is a part of the nervous system, surely a very important part, but still only a part. The cerebellum does function to compare the intended movement determined by the motor areas of the brain, namely the cerebrum and the basal ganglia with what is actually happening but does not accomplish this in a direct manner. The intention of movement is accomplished in the cerebrum and basal ganglia. If the intent of these motor areas is not being attained by skeletal muscles, the cerebellum detects that variation and sends feedback signals to the motor areas (cerebrum or basal ganglia) to either stimulate or inhibit the activity of the skeletal muscles. It is this **interaction** that helps to smooth and coordinate complex sequences of skeletal muscles' contractions. Note here that the cerebellum **does not directly send nerve impulses to skeletal muscles. It somehow has learned or remembers how to compare what is right or wrong concerning an intended movement.** This I find so totally amazing! **Ah, I'm sorry Big Cheese, you are going to make a mistake here! Error! Error!...and if the body is in harmony, balance, listening to all its organs, the error will be corrected. If not???**

POSTURE, POSTURE, POSTURE MELISSA! THINK ABOUT YOUR POSTURE!

An extremely important basic motor act or movement in our lives is posture...posture. The position of the body depends upon automatic muscle activity that counters the pull of gravity. When you are standing, the vestibular nuclei and certain other nuclei in the reticular formation of your brain transmit continuous messages into the spinal cord via the extrapyramidal tracts. (**The extrapyramidal pathway consists of all non-pyramidal neurons that transmit motor signals to the spinal cord that are mainly concerned with gross movements and posture**). The message transmitted down these tracts from the brain instruct the extensor muscles to stiffen the limb. Such muscle action opposes gravity and permits the limbs to support the body so that you do not fall over. Did you realize you are constantly running counter to the pull of gravity when standing? Well the body knows, and the degree of contraction of our limbs depends upon the organs and structures of our body in maintaining equilibrium.

Equilibrium is also balance, is also homeostasis in body language, so the body knows! The vestibular apparatus in the inner ear is one of the sense organs that receives information regarding equilibrium, and sends messages to the vestibular nuclei in the brainstem.

Within the nervous system, then, the cerebrum, cerebellum, basal ganglia, many parts of the brainstem, and the spinal cord are all involved in the complex regulation of body balance. Maintenance of posture provides a stable background against which intricate voluntary movements can take place.

POSTURE, AN EXTREMELY IMPORTANT MOTOR ACT IN CEREBRAL PALSY

Posture is the position of the body at any given time and this posture or the body attitudes that posture represents, are of utmost importance in the diagnosis of movement and posture. Because of their brain injuries, children with cerebral palsy may be unable to hold their head, trunk, arms, or legs in proper alignment against gravity, in one or many postures. Also, children with cerebral palsy often cannot move one body part independently of another, as in moving the whole head and shoulders along with the eyes, simply to accomplish looking to the right. With brain injury there is an inability for postures to be maintained against the pull of gravity.

There are several important postures, or positions that children need to master in order to acquire gross motor skills. These include: 1. supine (on the back), 2. prone (on the front), 3. sitting, 4. side-lying, 5. kneeling, 6. half-kneeling, and 7. standing. The motor skills that enable children to move from one place to another usually develop in a specific sequence. Before babies can master the more advanced movements, they <u>must</u> acquire the transitional movements that enable them to connect one posture to another. For babies with cerebral palsy, abnormal muscle tone makes many transitional movements difficult or impossible.

We are rarely aware of our posture maintenance, as we are also for the most part, unaware of the workings of our skeletal muscles that maintain body posture. Yet, these muscles function almost continuously making one tiny adjustment after another that enables us to maintain an erect or seated posture, despite the never-ending downward pull of gravity. This wonderful, amazing body just seems to know what has to be done without our concentrating on any aspect of it once we master the skill of sitting, standing, running, walking, etc. etc.

FOR VOLUNTARY MOVEMENT TO OCCUR, AS IT DOES IN POSTURE, EACH ELEMENT WITHIN THE NERVOUS SYSTEM MUST WORK IN HARMONY. MELISSA JUST COULD NOT PULL IT ALL TOGETHER IN HARMONY

"Failure of smooth progression of movements," has long been a problem for Melissa. Even as a baby I would test her reflexes if she was sitting to see if she could right herself if I pushed ever so slightly on her shoulder to the right or to the left. I didn't really understand what it was accomplishing for Melissa at the time, but as the unusual motor patterns, or sequences of movements were becoming ever more obvious, apparently checking her degree of "normal" movements kept us closer to an observation of the norm for Melissa. There is such a wide range of what is considered to be "normal" development, that is perhaps why it is so difficult to get a diagnosis of cerebral palsy early on. A child may have normal abilities in some areas, variable skills in other areas, or slower maturation and development in still other areas. So much depends on the individual child and their individual strengths and weaknesses.

For children with cerebral palsy, how they do the things they can do is probably more important than when they do them. The rapidity with which a child acquires skills does not matter as much as how well they are able to do them.

One doctor answered my questions concerning Melissa's difficulty in picking up motor skills in this way, "It is very difficult to make predictions, or know long term effects in children with a motor movement disorder because of the plasticity of a child's central nervous system." This apparently means that the brains of very young children have a much greater capacity to repair themselves than do adult brains. A child's nervous system produces many more brain cells and connections than are needed and eventually incorporated for use in the complex motor

73

tasks, and so if a brain injury occurs early, the undamaged areas of a child's brain can and sometimes will take over some of the functions of the damaged areas. Keeping one's eye on the norm, then, wasn't as far fetched an idea of mine as it sometimes seemed to others. I've learned that as a child's nervous system organizes over time damage to the brain may affect the child's motor abilities inversely meaning they may go in the positive direction, not necessarily always downward or in the negative direction. I so feared the worst each and every day for so long. Now I take it a day at a time, but that takes time and patience to learn how to live that way. A day at a time!

A NEUROLOGIC DISORDER CAN BE MANIFESTED IN LACK OF IMPULSE CONTROLAS SEEN WHEN MELISSA LIVES IN THE MINUTE, NOT THE DAY

Impulse control is not high on Melissa's list of strengths. If her body feels sick or out of sorts in any way, she expects me to "fix it" **now,** and that means immediately. Patience is <u>not</u> one of her virtues. We learned years ago not to tell her of any impending plans as she couldn't understand tomorrow or three weeks from now. Even with her calendar in front of her with the days marked off, she has no real concept of a time frame. She has a difficult time waiting, as all young children do, but her difficulty is immense in comparison with a normal child. She also has immense difficulty with the word NO. In that respect her "want it now" attitude reminds me of the terrible two's you hear so much about. They too, cannot take NO for an answer.

The nervous system, along with the endocrine system are the body's main communication systems. These two systems collectively organize and control the activities we know of as human behavior. In my mind, Melissa's body seems to be in a constant ready mode in a low hum setting, so at any time with no real rhyme or reason, in the long term to her behavior, she will react or over-react. Little thought processing seems to be involved and definitely a low point of reasoning with her mind. Simply the here and now, and I do mean **now.** I don't know any medical reason or explanation for this lack of impulse control. What I mean by this is that I have had to learn to deal with this aspect of her behavior by using my own common sense and parenting sense I have learned over the years, as nothing the professionals tell me seems to work.

I do know from years of experience with my daughter that there is little reasoning with my daughter in the logical sense of the word. Melissa reacts to stimuli in her own focused way, through her **own vision of reality.**

For example, a friend arrived to visit us from England. He was a counselor at a camp Melissa attended one year and has written letters to her as a pen pal. A very kindly gesture on his part, but certainly nothing romantic about any of it. She is certainly not invited to return to England with him, but she has been packing now for two days to return to England with him. Hopefully this dream, or vision, or compulsion, too shall pass, but it will have to pass of its own volition. Nothing anyone can say to her will have much effect on her thinking process. I do know that looking at it as if she cannot help her behavior, or stop it, or change it, has helped me greatly to have patience with her, and, at least, somewhat understand where in the world she is coming from.

SENSING THE WORLD: SOME BASIC PRINCIPLES

Each of us comes equipped with sensitivities that enable us to survive and thrive. We sense only a portion of the sea of energy that surrounds us. Our absolute threshold for any stimulus is the minimum stimulation necessary for us to detect it. Signal detection researchers report that our individual thresholds vary with our psychological state. How does the world out there get represented inside our heads? Put another way, how are the external stimuli that strike our bodies transformed into messages that our brains comprehend?

Perception is the process of organizing and interpreting sensory information, enabling us to recognize meaningful objects and events. Sensation is the process by which our sense receptors and nervous system receive and represent stimulus energies from our environment. People, temporarily, or permanently, deprived of one or more of their senses typically compensate by becoming more acutely aware of information from another working sense. Temporary experiences of sensory restriction often evoke a heightened awareness of all forms of sensation, but research shows that conflict between visual and other sensory information is usually resolved with the mind accepting the visual data, a tendency researchers call **visual capture**. I take all that to mean that what Melissa sees is what she believes. This man arrived all the way from England to see her and this meant in her mind that he perceived her in the same light that she perceived him. With the limited reasoning ability Melissa has, due to her mental retardation, she simply has great difficulty in adapting to the demands of life which go beyond the immediate, whether in the visual sense, auditory sense, or kinesthetic sense of her body.

MELISSA'S LACK OF IMPULSE CONTROL: A PART OF HER PATTERN OF IMPAIRED NEUROLOGICAL FUNCTIONING, AND LACK OF INTEGRATION OF HER NERVOUS SYSTEM

What I was learning to observe most of all was Melissa's pattern of neurological functioning. I was learning to become an expert on Melissa and her nervous system. To know and understand what she needed, how I could help her myself, and when we all needed outside help. In other words, I was learning and becoming determined to have my own perceptions of Melissa. Only in this way could I make sure she always knew how much she was loved, wanted, and accepted, despite, and in spite, of her sometimes big and sometimes little differences. **Cerebral palsy doesn't go away!** It's not like the common cold. Cerebral palsy is brain damage. It's something you have to learn to live with day by day.

The long-range ramifications of early insult, or injury, to the brain and nervous system depends to a great extent on which particular system is damaged and the degree of plasticity versus rigidity that particular neurological system has. **Among the functional neural systems that are believed to be least plastic, the motor pathways rank quite high.** As a result, it seems reasonable to assume that if the injury is in the motor pathway, there is less leeway for the remaining cells to develop the necessary networks for normal motor function. However, the phenomena of changing signs in young children with cerebral palsy points to the probability that some reorganization of neuromotor cells **must** be taking place in the presence of previously damaged neurons. As one doctor put it:

> "The relative homogeneity of developmental neuromotor problems, in contrast to the heterogeneity of neuromotor disorders acquired after the neuromotor systems have matured, may be due in part to a tendency of the young

damaged neuromotor systems to become organized in relatively homogeneous manners subsequent to lesions."

I took all that to mean that there was always hope that Melissa could, and would, reorganize her brain with time, help, and much love.

A CRASH COURSE IN ANATOMY, PHYSIOLOGY, NEUROPHYSIOLOGY, PSYCHOLOGY AND SOCIOLOGY

Learning to understand the Latin and Greek the doctors were speaking in was perhaps the most difficult learning task for my husband and I. To read and even try to understand the medical reports, and hopefully not appear a total idiot when confronted with yet another term that we were unfamiliar with, was a real stretching mental exercise for both my husband and myself. Actually it took us years to realize how well we did when we were taking a crash course in anatomy, physiology, neurophysiology, psychology and sociology all at the same time and all through Melissa's body. We didn't have a variety of textbooks and instructors. We did not have the luxury of learning one subject at one time. We had to learn it all lumped together in one subject title, cerebral palsy. Also a crash course, with no degree to go with it, and no grade, so you never knew how you were doing. No one ever, to my knowledge, affirmed how devoted and caring we were for our daughter. Looking back over the last twenty five years, I can now see what a great job we have done, but approval and recognition of our daily struggle would have been helpful.

Coming to grips with the idea that it was the brain via the whole nervous system that was causing the movement difficulty in Melissa's body was a hard concept to fully comprehend. The brain and spinal cord include several different motor systems, each of which can simultaneously control particular kinds of movements. For example, a person can walk and talk with a friend simultaneously. While doing so, he or she can gesture with the hands to emphasize a point, scratch an itch, brush away a fly, wipe perspiration off his or her forehead, and so on. Walking, postural adjustments, talking, movement of the arms and fingers, all involve different specialized motor systems. Since movements can be initiated by several means, and because there is no single cause of behavior, it is very difficult or nearly impossible to find a <u>single</u> starting point in the search for the neural mechanisms that control movement.

The final common pathway, however, of many neurologic disorders is known to be musculoskeletal dysfunction. Individuals with these disorders are prone to impaired postural reflexes, functional losses from weakness, and mental and emotional depression of the individuals. These functional neurological losses can be seen in such acts as: 1. smiling, 2. walking, 3. feeling angry, 4. being motivated, 5. having an idea, and 6. remembering a long-past event. Some of these experiences which are attributed, in general, to the "mind" are somehow related to the integrated activities of nerve cells in the body, either on a conscious level or an unconscious level.

LEARNING TO WALK...CONSCIOUS LEVEL OR SUBCONSCIOUS LEVEL?

I can voluntarily decide that I want to go for a walk, but usually I do not have to consciously think about the specific sequence of movements that will have to be performed to accomplish this intentional act. In the same way, much of voluntary activity is actually involuntarily regulated.

Unstable posture is a symptom characteristic of cerebellar dysfunction. Persons with cerebellar damage walk awkwardly, with the feet well apart, and they can have such difficulty maintaining balance that their gait appears drunken. Since an important function of the cerebellum is to provide appropriate timing for each succeeding movement, this loss of timing capability (which basically is the subconscious ability to predict ahead of time how far the different parts of the body will move in a given time), the person with cerebral palsy becomes unable to determine when the next movement should begin. As a result, the succeeding movement may begin too early or, more likely, too late. Therefore, complex movements of posture: sitting, standing, walking, running, even writing and talking, lack the orderly sequence from one movement to the next in progression.

We do know that all activities of the cerebellum are below the level of consciousness. The main function of the cerebellum is that of a reflex center through which coordination and refinement of muscular movements are affected, and by which changes in muscle tone and strength of muscle contraction are related to maintaining posture and equilibrium. As was stated previously in our writings, the cerebellum maintains proper positioning of the body in space, but this function is on a subconscious level of coordination of motor activity or movement.

The role of the cerebellum in programming movements can best be appreciated when seeing its absence in individuals with cerebellar disease. These individuals <u>cannot</u> perform movements smoothly. They **cannot start or stop movements quickly or easily.** If they are asked to rotate the wrist over and back rapidly, their motions are slow and irregular. They also cannot easily combine the movement of several joints into a single smooth, coordinated motion. To move the arm, they might first move the shoulder, then the elbow, and finally the wrist. A lot of work and energy to accomplish what you or I could do without even giving it a thought. In the blinking of an eye those of us with normal or healthy cerebellums accomplish a miracle each time we move in a fluid, balanced manner, without even realizing the beauty of it all. How often do we even give it a thought? How often do we give our normal body functioning a thought, or even a simple thank you?

HOW DID MELISSA ACCOMPLISH AS MUCH MOVEMENT AS SHE HAS WITHOUT A DEVELOPED CEREBELLUM?

If Melissa's cerebellum had never grown, as the MRI was testimony of, how in the world has she accomplished as much movement as she has in the last twenty five years? Damage to the cerebellum can cause the hand to swing around wildly unable to connect with its target, yet Melissa's hands and arms are very strong. She is basically able to use them for most of her daily care. Yes, the food gets tossed around on the table, but she does feed herself. Individuals with cerebellar disease also have oscillating, to-and-fro tremors that accompany their jerky movements when attempting to touch an object, and some of Melissa's difficulty in feeding herself, to be sure, is a result of this type of motion.

82

One doctor explained the function of the cerebellum to me in this way:

> "The cerebellum can be compared to the control system of an automatic pilot. It continually compares the higher brain's intention with the body's actual performance, and sends out messages to initiate the appropriate corrective measures. In this way, it helps promote smooth voluntary movements that are precise and economical in terms of muscular effort. Cerebellar injury results in loss of muscle tone, and clumsy, disorganized movements like Melissa's result."

Clumsy, disorganized I could handle. I know clumsy. I can be clumsy. I could handle the word clumsy easier than I could handle all the big words I had a difficult time pronouncing or comprehending.

THE BUILDING OF THE BRAIN: CHARACTERISTICS
OF NERVOUS TISSUE

I like how the Time Life book, "*The Brain*," explained the building of a brain. It stated, "The story of the human brain begins at the start of life itself. Only three weeks after the first cell division of conception, a tiny sheet of cells appears on the back of the minute embryo and grows at a feverish rate, creating millions of new brain cells each day. From this moment until death, the brain will undergo constant change as its fourteen billion nerve cells, called neurons, first create the increasingly complex interconnections that typify the healthy, adult brain, then start to die off and lose some of those vital connections as they age. During gestation, the brain grows into a two-thirds-sized likeness of its adult self. At birth its anatomy is virtually complete, but there is still work to be done. Every neuron must set out to make connections with others of its kind, and each cell must be wrapped in its own insulating material. These branching connectors and the insulating sheaths are responsible for the increasing weight and size of the brain in the growing child."

The cells of the cortex move apart and thus create enough room for the extra weight and volume of the maturing brain. Neural connections become increasingly more complicated as the brain matures. In the cortex alone each cell is estimated to have as many as 10,000 connections, making the possible connections in one human cortex about 200,000 times the population of the Earth. Everything rests on the precision of these contacts - motor coordination, perception, the retention of memories, the acquisition of a vocabulary, and the ability to develop patterns of thought but -- this is not a passive process. External environment and stimuli cause many of these pathways to be forged. Genes and outside influences act together to create each unique brain, and deprivation of any sort, sensory or emotional, can distort the growth of the brain. The brain-building processes of childhood form the basis for the refined perception and exquisite motor control necessary to operate in the adult world.

The two outstanding characteristics of nervous tissues are **excitability and conductivity.**

1. Excitability refers to the sensitivity of living beings to changes in their environment; the ability to adapt effectively and to be affected then by such changes constitutes excitability.

This property is highly developed in our receptor nerve endings. If our nervous system loses this excitability, life soon ends, as the body is unaware of harmful surroundings. Consequently, excitability is a valuable asset so far as preservation of life is concerned.

2. Conductivity is the property of nerve fiber to conduct an impulse, or in other words, how the brain is informed of changes in the environment. When the brain is informed of such changes it can then assign duties to various effector parts of the body. No change is visible in a nerve fiber as it conducts an impulse, but certain facts are known about conduction through research:

> A. The impulse is self-propagating. Each section of nerve fiber is affected in such a way, as it conducts an impulse, that it acts as a stimulus for the next section, and also furnishes the energy to transmit the impulses along.

> B. The impulse travels at a definite speed depending on the size of the nerve fiber over which it passes. Larger fibers conduct faster than smaller ones. In humans the impulses travel a fraction of a millimeter in the smallest nerve fibers, and 120 meters per second in the largest nerve fibers. This is a slower rate than that which sound waves travel, but even in a man six feet

tall, the impulses could travel in large nerve fibers from toes to brain and back to toes over large fibers, in less than one twentieth of a second.

C. Chemical changes occur in nerve fibers while they are conducting impulses. There is a larger use of oxygen, and greater production of carbon dioxide, than when they are not conducting. Glucose is used during conduction, and some ammonia is produced, but explanations of chemical changes that fully accompany activity in nerve fibers are not as well worked out as for skeletal muscle. We do know however, that for normal activity the brain is as dependent on glucose as on oxygen.

D. Thermal changes accompany conduction of impulses in nerves. The amount of heat produced is very small; it is less than one ten-thousandth of that produced in an equal weight of muscle by one contraction. In other words you will never become overheated from thinking, as you might from vigorous exercise.

E. Electrical changes accompany the passage of nerve impulses. If each section of nerve fiber is considered a battery, there is an infinite number of batteries discharging, as an impulse passes along from the inside to the outside of the axis cylinder, and a movement of sodium ions in the opposite direction during conduction of impulses. We also know that neurons are highly irritable, responsive to stimuli.   When a neuron is adequately stimulated, an electrical impulse is conducted along the length of its axon. Since the human body as a whole is electrically neutral; meaning it has the same number of positive and negative charges, we also know that there are sites where one type of charge predominates, making such regions positively or negatively charged. When opposite charges come together, energy is liberated that can be used to do work.

A number of chemical and physical factors can impair the conduction of impulses. Although their mechanism of action differ, alcohol, sedatives, and anesthetics all block nerve impulses. Cold and continuous pressure interrupt blood circulation (and hence the delivery of oxygen and nutrients) to the neuronal processes, impairing their ability to conduct impulses. For example, your fingers get numb when you hold an ice cube for more than a few seconds. Likewise, when you sit on your foot, it "goes to sleep." When you remove the pressure, the impulses begin to be transmitted once again, leading to an unpleasant prickly feeling.

After a nerve fiber conducts one impulse, a short interval of time must pass before it can conduct another. This period is called the refractory period. No stimulus, however strong, can force the nerve fiber to conduct a second impulse <u>before</u> it has recovered from the effects of the first. The recovery period is short, but **essential!**

Unlike the cells of epithelial tissue, neurons have only limited powers of regeneration, that is, a natural ability to renew themselves. Around six months of age, nerve cells lose their ability to reproduce. **Thus when a neuron is damaged or destroyed, it cannot be replaced by other neurons. A neuron destroyed is permanently lost, and only some types of damage may be repaired. The amount of excitability and conductivity in your nervous system remains a constant throughout your life!**

Another important factor in impulse conduction is the fact that there is only **one-way impulse conduction,** from a presynaptic axon to a post-synaptic cell. This is because only synaptic (a junction between the cells), end bulbs of presynaptic neurons can release neurotransmitters. As a result, <u>nerve impulses must move forward over their pathways.</u> **They cannot back up into another presynaptic neuron, a situation that would seriously disrupt homeostasis. One-way impulse conduction is crucial in preventing nerve impulse conduction along improper pathways....**

THE CEREBELLUM CAN, HOWEVER, "LEARN TO CORRECT MOTOR ERRORS"

The **purkinje cells** in the cerebellum can "learn" to correct motor errors. Typically, when a person first performs a new motor act, the degree of motor enhancement provided by the cerebellum to the agonist contraction, the degree of inhibition of the antagonist, and the timing of the offset are all almost always incorrect for precise performance of the movement. What does all that mean?

To begin with, the set of muscles that furnishes the power for the movement is referred to as the agonists. The other set, which by virtue of the muscle tone contributes to the smooth, even movements characteristic of voluntary activity, is known as the antagonists. Therefore muscular activity that results in movement or work involves two sets of muscles that act in varying degrees, in opposition to one another. So, when a person first performs a new motor act, the degree of motor enhancement, the degree of inhibition, and the timing of the offset, are not precise as to the performance of the movement. In other words, most motor acts **need practice, that means for everyone!**

However, after the motor act has been performed (practiced) many times, these individual sequential events become progressively more precise in performing the movement exactly, or close to exactly, the desired act, sometimes requiring only a few movements before the desired result is achieved, and at other times requiring literally hundreds of movements. In other words, we are better at some motor acts than others, and that means everyone, but practice does move an individual towards perfection, or at least some measure of it. There still remains the fact, however, that there are some motor acts, or moves, or skills, I would find it difficult to ever get accomplished at. In this context however, we are simply talking about the basic motor movements needed in everyday life, to get through the day in an independent fashion.

A DOCTOR AT COURAGE CENTER SAID: "MELISSA MAY NEVER WALK, YOU KNOW!"

Yes, we went to **Courage Center** too. The first time Melissa was seen there, this kindly doctor told us that she may never walk. **This is an extremely hard and difficult thing for most parents to accept.** I cried all the way home, but, of course, my husband said again, "There's no way they know that now; when she is just a baby." Thank heavens someone doesn't cry and stays in denial, so that the world keeps on turning. If everyone cried when reality hit too close to home not much would get done, would it? At the same time, we were slowly realizing that Melissa was having difficulty remaining in an upright position against the pull of gravity, and so could not sit unsupported, could not walk without her walker. We <u>were</u> looking at a wheelchair being her legs and mode of transportation. This was another hard pill to swallow, just like mental retardation and cerebral palsy...

In order to stand, we must keep our center of gravity above our feet, or we will fall. As we stand we tend to oscillate back and forth and from side to side. Our vestibular sacs and our visual system play an important role in the maintenance of posture. However, these systems are aided by the activity of the monosynaptic stretch reflex. When a person begins to lean forward, the large calf muscle is stretched and this stretching elicits compensatory muscular contraction that pushes the toes down, thus restoring upright posture. This is a function that Melissa cannot do now or has ever been able to do. We had Melissa to a reflexologist who would have her lay on the floor with her feet against the wall and push off with her toes. The purpose of this exercise, as it was explained to us, was to help give her the balance to stand which she lacked. To put it more simply, **her toes do not grab, they seem to stay "put" in a prone position!** I have always believed that this dysfunction of her toes has a great deal to do with her balance and her inability to stand.

The muscle spindles are very sensitive to changes in muscle length: they will increase their rate of firing when the muscle is lengthened by a very small amount. The interesting thing is that this detecting mechanism is adjustable. **When the muscle spindles are relaxed, they are relatively insensitive to stretch. However, when the gamma motor neurons are active they become shorter, and hence become much more sensitive to changes in muscle length. This property of adjustable sensitivity simplifies the role of the brain in controlling movement. The more control that can occur in the spinal cord, the fewer adjustments necessary from higher centers of the nervous system, and basically fewer messages must be sent to and from the brain.**

THE HUMAN BODY HAS LITERALLY THOUSANDS OF CONTROL SYSTEMS!

Yes, the human body has literally thousands of control systems in it. Most control systems of the body act by **negative feedback,** which can best be explained by describing the homeostatic control system in regulation of the carbon dioxide concentration in our body. A high concentration of carbon dioxide in the extracellular fluid increases pulmonary ventilation. This, in turn, decreases carbon dioxide concentration because the lungs then excrete greater amounts of carbon dioxide out of the body. In other words, the high concentration causes a decreased concentration, which is **negative** to the initiating stimulus. Conversely, if the carbon dioxide concentration falls too low, this causes a feedback increase in the concentration. This response also is negative to the initiating stimulus. Therefore, in general, if some factor becomes excessive or deficient, a control system initiates **negative feedback, which consists of a series of changes that return the factor toward a certain mean value, thus maintaining homeostasis.**

The term **homeostasis** is used by physiologists to mean, "maintenance of static or constant conditions in the internal environment." Essentially all of the organs and tissues of the body perform functions that help to maintain these constant conditions. The very fact that we remain alive is almost beyond our own control, for hunger makes us seek food, fear makes us seek refuge, and sensations of cold make us provide warmth for our bodies. Many are the forces that are impinging on us each and every day which we accomplish almost without thinking about it.

Our master control system, "The Big Cheese", as I like to call our brain, directs so many functions of our body of which we are not totally aware. As I stated previously, The major function of the nervous system is to process incoming information in such a way that appropriate motor responses (output) occur. When the important sensory information has been selected, it is then channeled into proper motor regions of the brain to cause the desired responses. This **channeling of information is called the integrative function of the nervous system.**

SCIENTISTS HAVE FOUND THAT NO PART OF THE BRAIN OPERATES IN TOTAL ISOLATION FROM ALL OTHER PARTS

Scientists have found that no part of the brain operates in total isolation from all the other parts of the brain. Virtually every research experiment seems to reveal interconnections, and the cerebellum, or little brain as it is often called, is no exception. So, I kept hoping that some other part of the brain would take over for the part that was damaged in my baby's brain. Actually, now I realize what a miracle she really has been, but at times I wanted her to be "normal" over night. I wanted to wake up and find this all to be a bad dream. I wanted my little girl to be able to grow up and have all the chances other little girls have. To run, to dance, to marry and have children. So, yes, I was looking for a miracle. Little did I realize that one was materializing right before my eyes each and every day.

Shock does strange things to one's mind I have learned. The shock of an actual loss, or an impending loss, all seem to affect the mind in the same way. Worry becomes your constant companion, but the worry is not a directed worry; it is just worry. Like a numb finger, your mind doesn't connect information with the rest of your body. Just as when the circulation is cut off from a numb finger, the information flow when you are in shock seems somewhat the same. You hear what the doctors and nurses are saying to you, but the information really doesn't take shape. It just seems to circle around in your head with no real goal. I was looking for an answer that would last for years, I know now. Now I know the only answers are daily ones realized in living out the day and finding the humor somehow, the love somehow, the caring somehow, that everyone needs to "have a good day." I have come to often resent those simple words said so easily today. They somehow make life seem so simple, so uncomplicated, so easy, so superficial. The choice is up to you everyone says, life is what you make it. **Choose to be happy.** I could go on and on with the simple answers I was hearing all around me. The tough answers came in the minutes and hours and days of learning how to live with cerebral palsy, and my beautiful daughter Melissa changing and aging day by day long before she should have. How hard she works each and every day to do the simple things everyone else takes so for granted. My precious, brave, beautiful Melissa who blows me a kiss as she goes off on her electric cart and says, "ov'wa'."

THE CLASSIFICATION SYSTEM USED IN DIAGNOSING THE TYPE OF CEREBRAL PALSY BY PROFESSIONALS

The classification system the doctors and other professionals use to identify the three broad types of cerebral palsy, based on the location of brain injury, is as follows:

1. pyramidal (spastic) cerebral palsy
2. extrapyramidal (choreo-athetoid) cerebral palsy
3. mixed-type cerebral palsy

Understanding these labels and classification systems is extremely important for the lay person to get a grasp on, as all services depend on the level of function or dysfunction the child has that is noted by the professionals. Incumbent in this classification of types of cerebral palsy is the understanding of the term **muscle tone...**

Muscle tone refers to the amount of tension or resistance to movement in a muscle. Muscle tone is what enables us to keep our bodies in a certain position or **posture.** For example, to sit with our backs straight and our heads up. Muscle tone, or more precisely, changes in muscle tone is what enables us to move. To bend your arm, to bring your hand up to your face, you must shorten, or increase the tone of the biceps muscles on the front of your arm, at the same time you are lengthening or reducing the tone of the triceps muscles on the back of your arm. Think about that the next time you simply scratch your nose. **Think about all the parts of the process that go on without your thinking about it.** Actually, when you do stop and think about it, it becomes harder to do, at least in your own particular natural way.

To complete a movement smoothly, the tone in all muscle groups involved **must be balanced.** The brain **must** send messages to each muscle group to actively change its resistance. **All children with cerebral palsy have damage to the area of the brain that controls muscle tone.** As a result, they may have increased muscle tone, reduced muscle tone, or a combination of the two (variable or fluctuating tone). **Which parts of their bodies are affected by the abnormal muscle tone depends upon where the brain damage occurs....**

TYPES, TYPES, LABELS, LABELS, CEREBRAL PALSY TYPES AND LABELS

The spastic type is apparently the most common and affects about half of all children with cerebral palsy. Children with this type have one or more tight muscle groups which limit movement. They may also have exaggerated stretch reflexes, ankle clonus, contractures, persistent primitive reflexes, and a positive Babinski. Good heavens! It sounded like Melissa could end up like an abstract painting, all out of shape with an odd form.

Then, of course, there was the extra-pyramidal or choreo-athetoid type of cerebral palsy. Roughly one quarter of children with cerebral palsy have this type, I was told. It is caused, they seemed to be certain of, by damage to the cerebellum or basal ganglia. Damage to these areas may cause, I was told, a child to develop involuntary, purposeless movements often interfering with speaking, feeding, reaching, grasping, and other skills requiring coordinated movements. I was also told that this type involved involuntary grimacing and tongue thrusting which may lead to swallowing problems, drooling, and slurred speech. **Oh, this is wonderful, now I thought, no longer an abstract painting that at least would just stay put, now the painting was going to be moving all over the wall!**

The mixed-type of cerebral palsy did give me some hope. Apparently about one quarter of children with cerebral palsy have both the spastic muscle tone of pyramidal cerebral palsy and the involuntary movement of extrapyramidal cerebral palsy. This is true, I was told, because they have injuries to **both** the pyramidal and extrapyramidal areas of the brain. Somehow the implications of that information didn't really sink into my thinking in the way it should have. I looked at the mixed-type as a kind of blessing, a relief in a way, maybe a diversion from sameness?

The spasticity effect is caused by increased muscle tone, also called high tone, or hypertonia. With high tone the movements will be stiff and awkward, because the muscles are too "tight," and their tone is not balanced. I can handle that, I thought, "We can work on balance with Melissa, we can somehow 'loosen her up.'"

With low tone the children will have trouble maintaining positions without support, because the muscles do not contract enough and are too relaxed. It is difficult for children with low tone to remain upright against the pull of gravity in positions such as sitting and standing. As a result, a child with low tone usually sits leaning forward, with a **rounded back.** I can handle that I thought, "We'll just have to tighten Melissa up when she gets too 'loose.'" I was fluctuating as much as Melissa's muscle tone was.

The fluctuating tone simply means these children will have a combination of high and low tone. **This child may have low muscle tone when at rest, and then increase to high tone with active movement.** Sounded a lot like me when I was resting versus being active. So once again I thought, "I can handle that," and decided in my mind that Melissa would simply have to learn to be active when she was at rest and resting when she was active. **Confusion abounds when labels are placed on tables.**

Were the labels, the names, confusing me even more than I already was? It took me a long time to realize that everything I was learning each and every day from Melissa actually meant more to me than anything anyone else could ever tell me. As my nurse friend would always say, "Listen to the patient, watch the patient." You'll learn all you need to know if you just pay close attention to who you're attending to. **"What you cannot learn from observation or listening, you must learn by asking the right questions. If you ask the right questions, you always get the right answers."**

THE NERVOUS SYTEM: THE ACTIVATING MECHANISM OF THE TOTAL BODY

In summary, since the nervous system is the activating mechanism of the total body, none of the body's systems function without adequate performance of the nervous system. The capability of the central nervous system to react to environmental influences; to receive

96

and conduct nerve impulses; to interpret, store, integrate, and process information; and to activate responses is essential to life and learning itself.

We know that the cerebellum is in charge of fine-tuned movement. The cerebellum coordinates the start, execution and end of a physical act, helps to maintain balance and body tone, and is crucial in performing rapid and consecutive movements. We also know that the cerebellum draws its raw data from "position-sense" receptors scattered throughout the body. Proprioception; the "sixth sense," informs the individual of limb position and muscle tension, relying on information from hundreds of thousands of stretch receptors buried in muscle and tendons. Sensitive to movement, the receptors report to the brain about the position of limbs and body through the **spinal cord.** The cerebellum then uses the data from the spinal cord to advise the motor cortex on its next move. What teamwork! What synchronization! What a marvelous human machine this body of ours is!

Rapid stretch of a muscle triggers the monosynaptic stretch reflex, a stumble triggers righting reflexes, and the rapid approach of an object toward the face causes a startle response, a complex reflex consisting of several muscle groups. Other stimuli initiate sequences of movements that we have previously learned. The presence of food causes eating, and the sight of a loved one evokes a hug and a kiss.

Reflexes are simply circuits of sensory neurons, interneuron (usually), and efferent neurons that control simple responses to particular stimuli. A sudden lengthening of a muscle causes that muscle to contract, but the motor system of the brain will set the length of the intrafusal muscle fibers and increase their sensitivity to increases in muscle length and thereby control limb position.

It is an absolutely amazing process: When you put it all into slow motion, as manifested in and through our Melissa's body.

OPEN HEART, OPEN MIND, OPEN ARMS: ESSENTIAL INGREDIENTS OF LIVING WITH A HANDICAPPED CHILD

Melissa was born and I was filled with a feeling at that very moment, it was going to be a different kind of life from then on. Thank goodness I didn't know how different it was going to be. The challenges have been many, but the rewards even more numerous. I've learned to change what I can change in my life and Melissa's, and to let go of what cannot be changed. When the double diagnosis of mental retardation, and cerebral palsy came, I had no idea what either of them meant. It was all just words. Unable to fix her, I fixed the situation with **denial** for years. It was easier to **deny** than **fix**. I've learned that accepting the **truth** as early as possible is the best route to follow for the child and the parent.

I now fully comprehend that cerebral palsy is a brain problem, as I know also fully now that the brain controls body movements. The inability to understand that concept kept me from the full conceptual understanding that I could not **make** her walk. Therapy, exercise, and other forms of stimulation could not **make** her walk. I wanted her to walk. She wanted to walk. It has only been the last three or four years of Melissa's life that she doesn't repeat the words, "Maybe I walk someday Mom?" For years what kept all of us going was my favorite saying, **"Where there's a will there's a way."** I've learned sometimes, there's just the **will.** The way is woven into the symptoms and characteristics of the disability. Cerebral palsy is not a progressive disorder, but it is brain damage, and it is manifested as a static disorder in which the disorder or disability will not get worse. **"What you see is what you get."** Accept it for what it is as soon as possible and get on with life. **"Less is always better,"** my father would say to me. **"Going around in circles Bev, is like the dog trying to catch its own tail. It'll never happen."**

Melissa's cerebellum had never grown. That was a fact substantiated by an MRI at the age of 12. Collect the facts concerning your child's disability and learn from the facts what you need to know, and don't spend endless hours or years worrying about what could be. **Focus on what is!** Collect your miracles in the here and now, and live life to the fullest. The greatest **gift** any adult can give to a child, whether handicapped or not, is to take care of their needs and be committed to watching over them in a loving way. Sometimes loving unconditionally, as is necessary, particularly with a handicapped child, does not always come easy.

All parents at times wish they could "get away," or even "run away," at least for a little alone time. **Special needs children have such specialized and constant needs it is difficult, almost impossible, to leave them unsupervised for any length of time.**

Melissa is twenty five years old, and I still cannot leave her alone for a very long period without enormous concern. Last week I shopped for groceries, running down the aisles, frantically and hurriedly, to be sure I returned before her favorite movie on TV was finished. Out of sight, out of mind, is **never** true when you have a special needs child. They are always and forever vulnerable, and so are you.

I look at my daughter today through loving eyes, seeing always how strong she is in many ways, and how fragile she is at the same time. The most amazing part of all of this is knowing how much she strengthens all of us with her bravery.

With my first full realization of Melissa being afflicted with cerebral palsy I couldn't help but think, "How could this happen to us?" But now as I think back to the hard times and the good times, all I can really remember is

100

what in the world would life have been like without her? Nothing in life for anyone is easy, and certainly nothing is easy when it comes to cerebral palsy or any handicap, but as with all of life you learn to accept what is, enjoy the simpler things in life, and not take life so seriously. A sense of humor goes a long way each and every day.

I hope you have enjoyed reading our story of Melissa, cerebral palsy, and one family's learning to deal with the roll of the dice. Telling this story has been a real uplifting and learning experience for me, and I would hope it could help others look at the positive sides as well as the negative sides of living with a handicap of any kind. I would end with always try to look at what any individual, handicapped or not, can do, not what they cannot do. This means, "Accentuate the positive, thereby hopefully eliminating the negative."

Thank you,

Al and Bev Gelhaye

Al and Bev Gelhaye

PLAN FOR CHILD'S FUTURE NOW!

My personal twenty five year rewalk with cerebral palsy. Recommendations, changes, and what steps I would take if I could re-walk it.

Bev Gelhaye

Bev Gelhaye

Birth Process
1. Gynecologist: preferable for the birth which would directly have led to a pediatrician to assess Melissa.
2. Pediatrician: definitely for early neurologic assessment and diagnosis.
3. After Diagnosis: Ask for a social worker through the county you live in. They will help you find an Association for Retarded Citizens (ARC). They can get you the phone numbers needed to get you started.

Getting an Assessment-Recommendations
1. A developmental pediatrician is one who specializes in children with disabilities, and especially developmental disabilities.
2. A neurologist is one who specializes in diseases and disorders of the nervous system who may do one or more of the following:
   A. MRI to obtain a detailed picture of the child's brain.
   B. EEG to measure the electrical activity of the brain and identify if there is seizure activity.
   C. Cat Scan
   D. Head Sonogram which uses sound waves to visualize the structure of the brain.
3. An orthopedic surgeon is one who specializes in medical treatment and surgery of bones, tendons, ligaments and joints.

4.   A physiatrist is one who specializes in the evaluation and treatment of physical impairment. He has expertise in rehabilitation, and works closely with OT and PT (occupational therapy and physical therapy), helping direct the therapeutic process.

Therapists:
    1. Physical Therapist
    2. Occupational Therapist
    3. Speech Therapist
    4. Audiologist
    5. Nutritionalist

Early Intervention Program
    Begins before the age of three.

Pre-school Special Education Program.

This includes more than academic subjects (reading, writing, and arithmetic). It also includes therapeutic and other services aimed at helping children overcome delays in all areas of development. By law, a child's special education program <u>must</u> include all special services or related services.

Under Public Law 94-142 the Federal Government has to provide funds for the education of children with disabilities from age three beginning in 1991. In addition, Congress has established a program of grants to support states that offer early intervention services to children from birth. Check with your local association for retarded citizen program or United Cerebral Palsy, and also your local school district.
PLAN FOR YOUR CHILD'S FUTURE NOW!

ARC Minnesota
3225 Lyndale Avenue South
Minneapolis, MN 55408
(612) 827-5641, Toll free 1-800-582-5256

ARC of Hennepin County
Diamond Hill Center, Suite 140
4301 Highway 7
Minneapolis, MN 55416-5810
(6120 920-0755

West Hennepin Community Service
1001 Highway 6, #203
Hopkins, MN 55305
(612) 988-4177

ARC of Hennepin County is a private, non-profit agency providing advocacy and support to people with developmental disabilities and their families. ARC of Hennepin County is committed to securing for all people with developmental disabilities the opportunity to choose and realize their goals of where and how they learn, live, work, and play.

Programs and Services

A wide array of programs and services are offered to individuals with developmental disabilities to gain information, exchange resources and share common concerns.

- information about developmental disabilities resources and services
- one-to-one advocacy to obtain appropriate services
- individual and family counseling
- support groups for families, individuals and siblings

- workshops and training on issues like parenting, housing, education, and guardianship or conservatorship
- assistance with recreational referral and inclusion
- public policy education and advocacy

Volunteer Opportunities

ARC of Hennepin County was founded by and currently relies on volunteers. ARC of Hennepin County has an ongoing and short-term opportunities for individuals and groups to volunteer.

Membership

ARC of Hennepin County members are the driving force of our organization and help to develop the direction of programs and services. Join the nation's largest grassroots network making positive change in the lives of people with developmental disabilities and their families. Members can enjoy 50% off on ARC of Hennepin County workshops and town meetings, access to health and life insurance and current information from ARC of Hennepin and ARC state and national chapters.

For more information, call ARC of Hennepin County at 920-0855.

Pacer Center

4826 Chicago Avenue South
Minneapolis, MN 55417-1098
(612) 827-2966, Voice/TTY FAX (612) 827-3065
Toll free (800) 53 PACER for parents in greater Minnesota

Pacer's Mission
Pacer Center is a coalition of organizations founded on the concept of Parents Helping Parents. Pacer strives to improve and expand opportunities that enhance the quality of life for children and young adults with disabilities and their families.

Courage Center

3915 Golden Valley Road
Golden Valley, MN 55422
(612) 588-0811

Complete rehabilitation and independent living services for children and adults with physical disabilities and speech, hearing and vision impairments.

City of Bloomington
Parks and Recreation Division
Department of Community Services
Crystie Dufon, Adaptive Recreation Supervisor
2215 West Old Shakopee Road
Bloomington, MN
(612) 948-8877

Life Planning for Persons with Disabilities
9001 E. Bloomington Freeway #127
Bloomington, MN 55420
senior Partners:
Arnold Gruetzmacher
Daryll Stenburg
(612) 881-5339
Toll free (800) 487-5310
FAX (612) 881-5057

Fraser-Whitbeck School
2400 West 64th Street
Richfield, MN 55423
(612) 861-1688

Operated by a non-profit organization with a 58-year tradition of community services.

- Providing comprehensive early education and child care options for children with typical or special needs with a unique inclusive environment.
- Full and part-time services for children 6 weeks to 6 years of age.
- Licensed teachers.
- Medical rehabilitation services including occupational, physical, speech/language, and music therapy.
- Respite care services available to children with special needs.
- Family education and support services available.

Opportunity Partners, Inc.
5500 Opportunity Court
Minnetonka, MN 55343
(612) 938-5511
FAX (612) 930-4279
TDD (612) 930-4293

Opportunity Partners is a consumer driven community resource offering quality choices that prepare adults with developmental disabilities or traumatic brain injury for independence.

Faith and Light
Barbara Stevens, National Coordinator
RR 1, Joshua Cook Lane
Willfleet, Massachusetts 02667
(508) 349-2514

An international ecumenical association with mentally handicapped people, their families and friends. Faith and Light communities offer opportunities for friendship through the joys of being with one another. The simple beauty of Faith and Light grew from real life experiences and not just ideas. Faith and Light is a support system -

a way to build relationships. Our Faith and Light have been together three years. We named our group Family and Friends. We have between twenty five to thirty in our Family and Friends. We gather the first Sunday of the month and share a meal together and have fellowship. We celebrate everyone's birthday for that month and fun is had by all.

National Organizations

United Cerebral Palsy Associations, Inc.
7 Penn Plaza, Suite 804
New York, NY 10001
(212) 268-6655
(800) USA-1UCP (872-1827)

This federation has approximately two hundred state and local affiliates in the United States. Support services, information and referrals are available free to the public. A publications catalog is available.

American Academy for Cerebral Palsy & Developmental Medicine
P.O. Box 11086
Richmond, VA 23230-1086
(804) 282-0036

This organization of health-care providers offers referrals to the public.

International Organization

Canadian Cerebral Palsy Association (CCPA)
40 Dundas Street W. Suite 222
Toronto, Ontario M5G 2C2
Canada
(416) 979-7923

CCPA works to integrate persons with cerebral palsy into society through a variety of educational activities. It helps form support groups, distributes information, and makes referrals.

SHE DIDN'T CRY
Bibliography
Cerebral Palsy

1.   Cerebral Palsy/A Complete Guide For Caregiving
      Authors: Freeman Miller, M.D.
                    & Steven J. Bachrach, M.D.
                    With Marilyn L. Boos, R.N.C., Linda
                    Duffy, P.A.C.,
                    Douglas T. Pearson, Ph.D., Rhonda S.
                    Walter, M.D.,
                    & Joan Lenett Whinston

2.   Cerebral/Remediation of Communication Disorders
      Series
      Author: James C. Hardy, Ph.D.

3.   Children With Cerebral Palsy/A Parent's Guide
      Edited by Elaine Geralis
      Foreward by Tom Ritter

4.   Human Anatomy and Physiology/2nd Edition
      Author: Elaine N. Marieb, R.N., Ph.D.
                    pp. 378-422,484,533

5.   Textbook of Medical Physiology/9th Edition
      Authors: Arthur C. Guyton, M.D.
                    John E. Hall, Ph.D.
                    pp. 566-568, 702-703, 710-731

6.   Human Physiology/6th Edition/The Mechanisms of
      Body Function
      Authors: Arthur J. Vander, M.D.
                    James H. Sherman, Ph.D.
                    Dorothy S. Luciano, Ph.D.
                    pp. 348-368, 370-377

7. Principles of Anatomy and Physiology/7th Edition
    Authors: Gerard J. Tortora, B.S., M.A. Biology
                Sandra Reynolds Grabowski, B.S. Biology,
                Ph.D. Neurophysiology
                pp. 404-428, 439, 457-466, 439

8. Human Anatomy & Physiology/2nd Edition
    Authors: Eldra Pearl Solomon, Ph. D.
                Richard R. Schmidt, Ph.D.
                Peter James Adragna, Ph.D.
                pp. 433-473, 500-525

9. Human Physiology and Mechanisms of Disease/5th
    Edition
    Author: Arthur C. Guyton, M.D.
                pp. 416-419, 420-435, 331

10. Essentials of Human Anatomy & Physiology/4th
    Edition
    Author: John W. Hole, Jr.
                pp. 226-248

11. Introduction to the Human Body/The Essentials of
    Anatomy &   Physiology/3rd Edition
    Author: Gerard J. Tortora
                pp. 162, 225-234

12. Human Anatomy and Physiologoy/5th Edition
    Authors: Barry G. King, Ph.D.
                Mary Jane Showers, R.N., Ph.D.
                pp. 8-10, 87-95

13. Neuroscience in Medicine
    Editor: P. Michael Conn, Ph.D.
                pp. 213-225

14. Essentials of Human Anatomy & Physiology/4th
    Edition
    Author: Elaine N. Marieb, R.N., Ph.D.
                pp. 208, 229-235

15. Mind and Brain/Journey Through the Mind and Body
By the Editors of Time-Life Books

16. How Things Work/The Brain
Time-Life Books

17. Human Physiology From Cells to Systems
Author: Lauralee Sherwood, School of
             Medicine, West Virginia University
             pp. 126-157, 239-248

18. Diseases/Causes & Complications - Assessment Findings - Nursing Diagnoses & Interventions - Patient Teaching - Current Therapy
Springhouse Corporation Editors, Contributors and Consultants
             pp. 682-684

19. Technique of the Neurologic Examination/4th Edition
A Programmed Text By: William E. DeMyer, M.D.
             pp. 78-79, 282-308, 436-439

20. Better Homes and Gardens New Family Medical Guide
Edited by Edwin Kiester, Jr.
Illlustrations by Kelly Solis-Navarro and Evanell Towne
             pp. 122-130, 139, 140-143, 155-156

21. The New Illustrated Medical Encyclopedia & Guide to Family Health
Edited by Robert E. Rothenberg, M.D., F.A.C.S.
"Compiled and Prepared by Medbook Publications, Inc."
             pp. 364-365, 412-414, 359

22. <u>Mosby's Clinical Nursing/3rd Edition</u>
    Authors: June M. Thompson, R.N., M.S.,
                 Dr. P.H.
                 Gertrude K. McFarland, R.N., D.N.Sc.,
                 F.A.A.N.
                 Jane E. Hirsch, R.N., M.S.
                 Susan M. Tucker, R.N., M.S.N., Ph.N.
                 pp. 229-257

23. <u>Luckmann and Sorensen's Medical Surgical</u>
    <u>Nursing/A</u>   <u>Psychophysiologic Approach/4th</u>
    <u>Edition</u>
    Authors: Joyce M. Black, M.S.N., R.N., C.
                 Esther Matassarin-Jacobs, Ph.D.,
                 R.N., O.C.N.
                 pp. 617-635, 637-671

24. <u>Principles of Neural Science/3rd Edition</u>
    Edited by: Eric R. Kandel
                 James H. Schwartz
                 Thomas M. Jessell
                 Center for Neurobiology & Behavior
                 The Howard Hughes Medical
                 Institute & College of Physicians &
                 Surgeons of Columbia University
                 pp. 626-646

25. <u>Physiology of Behavior/5th Edition</u>
    Author: Neil R. Carlson, University of
                 Massachusetts
                 pp. 78-105, 226-251

26. <u>Physiology of Behavior/5th Edition</u>
    Author: Neil R. Carlson, University of
                 Massachusetts
                 pp. 74-1-5, 242-269

27. Neurological Rehabilitation/3rd Edition
Edited by: Darcy Ann Umphred, Ph.D., P.T.
Illustrated by: Steve Schmidt and Ben Burton with
50 contributors, and 362 illustrations by Mosby.
pp. 48-65, 66-80, 81-91, 263-286,
657-680

28. Neurology of the Newborn/3rd Edition
Author: Joseph J. Volpe, M.D., Harvard
Medical School
pp. 267,346-348,586-633

29. Neuroscience Nursing
Author: Ellen Barker, M.S.N., R.N., C.N.R.N.
President, Neuroscience Nursing
Consultants with 24 Contributors
and 36 Consultants
pp. 3-47, 49-92, 536-558, 655-667

30. Exceptional Children in the Schools/Special
Education in Transition/2nd Edition
Editor: Lloyd M. Dunn
pp. 65-78, 317, 467-478

31. The Psychology of Exceptional Children/3rd
Edition
Authors: Karl C. Garrison, Professor of
Education
Dewey G. Force, Asst. Professor of
Educational Psychology
pp. 366-389, 391-413

32. Human Development/4th Edition
Authors: Diane E. Papalia, University of
Pennsylvania
Sally Wendkis Olds
With: Ruth Duskin Feldman
pp. 116-126

33. Psychology/3rd Edition
    Author: David G. Myers
                Hope College
                Holland, Michigan
                Chapters 5 and 6

34. Physiology and Anatomy/7th Edition
    Author: Esther M. Greisheimer
                B.S. Education, M.A., Ph.D., M.D.
                With: Ann A Miruldo, R.N., B.S.
                pp. 243-255